DOMESDAY BOOK

Staffordshire

History from the Sources

DOMESDAY BOOK

A Survey of the Counties of England

LIBER DE WINTONIA

Compiled by direction of

KING WILLIAM I

Winchester
1086

DOMESDAY BOOK

A Survey of the Counties of England

LIBER DE WINTONIA

Compiled by direction of

KING WILLIAM I

Winchester
1086

DOMESDAY BOOK

text and translation edited by

JOHN MORRIS

24

Staffordshire

edited from a draft translation prepared by

Alison Hawkins and Alex Rumble

PHILLIMORE
Chichester
1976

History from the Sources
General Editor: John Morris

The series aims to publish history written directly from the sources for all interested readers, both specialists and others. The first priority is to publish important texts which should be widely available, but are not.

DOMESDAY BOOK

The contents, with the folio on which each county begins, are:

Domesday Book is termed *Liber de Wintonia* (The Book of Winchester) in column 332c

INTRODUCTION

The Domesday Survey

In 1066 Duke William of Normandy conquered England. He was crowned King, and most of the lands of the English nobility were soon granted to his followers. Domesday Book was compiled 20 years later. The Saxon Chronicle records that in 1085

> at Gloucester at midwinter ... the King had deep speech with his counsellors ... and sent men all over England to each shire ... to find out ... what or how much each landholder held ... in land and livestock, and what it was worth ... The returns were brought to him.[1]

William was thorough. One of his Counsellors reports that he also sent a second set of Commissioners 'to shires they did not know, where they were themselves unknown, to check their predecessors' survey, and report culprits to the King.'[2]

The information was collected at Winchester, corrected, abridged, chiefly by omission of livestock and the 1066 population, and fair-copied by one writer into a single volume. Norfolk, Suffolk and Essex were copied, by several writers, into a second volume, unabridged, which states that 'the Survey was made in 1086'. The surveys of Durham and Northumberland, and of several towns, including London, were not transcribed, and most of Cumberland and Westmorland, not yet in England, was not surveyed. The whole undertaking was completed at speed, in less than 12 months, though the fair-copying of the main volume may have taken a little longer. Both volumes are now preserved at the Public Record Office. Some versions of regional returns also survive. One of them, from Ely Abbey,[3] copies out the Commissioners' brief. They were to ask

> The name of the place. Who held it, before 1066, and now?
> How many hides?[4] How many ploughs, both those in lordship and the men's?
> How many villagers, cottagers and slaves, how many free men and Freemen?[5]
> How much woodland, meadow and pasture? How many mills and fishponds?
> How much has been added or taken away? What the total value was and is?
> How much each free man or Freeman had or has? All threefold, before 1066,
>   when King William gave it, and now; and if more can be had than at present?

The Ely volume also describes the procedure. The Commissioners took evidence on oath 'from the Sheriff; from all the barons and their Frenchmen; and from the whole Hundred, the priests, the reeves and six villagers from each village'. It also names four Frenchmen and four Englishmen from each Hundred, who were sworn to verify the detail.

The King wanted to know what he had, and who held it. The Commissioners therefore listed lands in dispute, for Domesday Book was not only a tax-assessment. To the King's grandson, Bishop Henry of Winchester, its purpose was that every 'man should know his right and not usurp another's'; and because it was the final authoritative register of rightful possession 'the natives called it Domesday Book, by analogy

---

[1] Before he left England for the last time, late in 1086. [2] Robert Losinga, Bishop of Hereford 1079-1095 (see *E.H.R.* 22, 1907, 74). [3] *Inquisitio Eliensis,* first paragraph. [4] A land unit, reckoned as 120 acres. [5] *Quot Sochemani.*

from the Day of Judgement'; that was why it was carefully arranged by Counties, and by landholders within Counties, 'numbered consecutively ... for easy reference'.[6]

Domesday Book describes Old English society under new management, in minute statistical detail. Foreign lords had taken over, but little else had yet changed. The chief landholders and those who held from them are named, and the rest of the population was counted. Most of them lived in villages, whose houses might be clustered together, or dispersed among their fields. Villages were grouped in administrative districts called Hundreds, which formed regions within Shires, or Counties, which survive today with minor boundary changes; the recent deformation of some ancient county identities is here disregarded, as are various short-lived modern changes. The local assemblies, though overshadowed by lords great and small, gave men a voice, which the Commissioners heeded. Very many holdings were described by the Norman term *manerium* (manor), greatly varied in size and structure, from tiny farmsteads to vast holdings; and many lords exercised their own jurisdiction and other rights, termed *soca*, whose meaning still eludes exact definition.

The Survey was unmatched in Europe for many centuries, the product of a sophisticated and experienced English administration, fully exploited by the Conqueror's commanding energy. But its unique assemblage of facts and figures has been hard to study, because the text has not been easily available, and abounds in technicalities. Investigation has therefore been chiefly confined to specialists; many questions cannot be tackled adequately without a cheap text and uniform translation available to a wider range of students, including local historians.

Previous Editions

The text has been printed once, in 1783, in an edition by Abraham Farley, probably of 1250 copies, at Government expense, said to have been £38,000; its preparation took 16 years. It was set in a specially designed type, here reproduced photographically, which was destroyed by fire in 1808. In 1811 ·and 1816 the Records Commissioners added an introduction, indices, and associated texts, edited by Sir Henry Ellis; and in 1861-1863 the Ordnance Survey issued zincograph facsimiles of the whole. Texts of individual counties have appeared since 1673, separate translations in the Victoria County Histories and elsewhere.

This Edition

Farley's text is used, because of its excellence, and because any worthy alternative would prove astronomically expensive. His text has been checked against the facsimile, and discrepancies observed have been verified against the manuscript, by the kindness of Miss Daphne Gifford of the Public Record Office. Farley's few errors are indicated in the notes.

[6] *Dialogus de Scaccario* 1,16.

The editor is responsible for the translation and lay-out. It aims at what the compiler would have written if his language had been modern English; though no translation can be exact, for even a simple word like 'free' nowadays means freedom from different restrictions. Bishop Henry emphasized that his grandfather preferred 'ordinary words'; the nearest ordinary modern English is therefore chosen whenever possible. Words that are now obsolete, or have changed their meaning, are avoided, but measurements have to be transliterated, since their extent is often unknown or arguable, and varied regionally. The terse inventory form of the original has been retained, as have the ambiguities of the Latin.

Modern English commands two main devices unknown to 11th century Latin, standardised punctuation and paragraphs; in the Latin, *ibi* ('there are') often does duty for a modern full stop, *et* ('and') for a comma or semi-colon. The entries normally answer the Commissioners' questions, arranged in five main groups, (i) the place and its holder, its hides, ploughs and lordship; (ii) people; (iii) resources; (iv) value; and (v) additional notes. The groups are usually given as separate paragraphs.

King William numbered chapters 'for easy reference', and sections within chapters are commonly marked, usually by initial capitals, often edged in red. They are here numbered. Maps, indices and an explanation of technical terms are also given. Later, it is hoped to publish analytical and explanatory volumes, and associated texts.

The editor is deeply indebted to the advice of many scholars, too numerous to name, and especially to the Public Record Office, and to the publisher's patience. The draft translations are the work of a team; they have been co-ordinated and corrected by the editor, and each has been checked by several people. It is therefore hoped that mistakes may be fewer than in versions published by single fallible individuals. But it would be Utopian to hope that the translation is altogether free from error; the editor would like to be informed of mistakes observed.

The Staffordshire text includes more local knowledge than usual. Samson, listed with the clergy of Wolverhampton, was probably the editor who compiled and wrote the Domesday Book at Winchester. Elsewhere he relied upon written returns alone, but Staffordshire includes lands which he held himself, with whose detail he was personally acquainted, as well as the holdings of his colleagues and neighbours.

The map was drawn by Jim Hardy.

Conventions

*	refers to a note.
[ ]	enclose words omitted in the MS.

( )   enclose editorial explanations.

246 a

IN BVRGO de *STADFORD* habet Rex in fuo dñio
xviii . burgenfes . 7 viii . uaftas manſ . Præter has hɫ
rex ibi . xxii . manſ de honore comitū . Harū . v . funt
uaftæ . aliæ inhabitantur.

Eᴘs de ceftre hɫ . xiiii . manſ . Vna . ē uafta.

Abbatia de Bertona . hɫ . v . manſ.

Rogeri coɱ hɫ . iii . manſ quæ jaceɴ ad halam ; Ipfe coɱ
hɫ inᵗ murum . xxxi . manſ . Ex his . x . funt uaftæ.

Hugo filius ej ten de comitatu . v . manſ . 7 ptiñ ad Guruelde;

Rotbt de Stadford hɫ xiii . manſ de honore comitū
7 ptiñ ad Bradelie . Ex his . vi . funt uaftæ.   ꟊ uaftæ
Idē Robt hɫ de feudo fuo . xli . manſ . Ex his . xvii . fuɴ

Witts . f . Anfculfi hɫ de comitatu . iiii . manſ . quæ ptiñ
ad Pennā ꟽ comiɫ . Ex his una tantm eft hofpitata.

de ferer'
Henricus hɫ . i . manſ uaftā . Prbi de burgo hñt . xiiii.

Hi oɱs hñt fachā 7 focha . Rex hɫ de oɱibꝫ geldū ꝑ anñ.

Tēpore regis . E . reddeb burgū de Stadford de oɱibꝫ
cſuetudinibꝫ . ix . lib denar . Duæ partes erant regis . tcia comit;
Modo hɫ rex . W . de reddit burgi . vii . lib . inᵗ fuā
parte 7 comitis . Medietate partis ꝓpriæ regis hɫ Robt
dono regis ut dicit.

STAFFORDSHIRE

B In The Borough of STAFFORD

*1 The King has 18 burgesses and 8 unoccupied dwellings in his
   lordship; besides these the King has 22 dwellings of the Earl's
   Honour; 5 of them are unoccupied, the others inhabited.

2 The Bishop of Chester has 14 dwellings; one is unoccupied.

3 Burton Abbey has 5 dwellings.

4 Earl Roger has 3 dwellings which lie in (Sheriff) Hales (lands).
   The Earl himself has 31 dwellings within the walls; 10 of
   them are unoccupied.

*5 His son Hugh holds 5 dwellings from the Earldom; they belong
   to Worfield.

6 Robert of Stafford has 13 dwellings of the Earl's Honour;
   they belong to Bradley(-by-Stafford); 6 of them are unoccupied.

7 Robert also has 41 dwellings of his own Holding; 17 of them
   are unoccupied.

8 William son of Ansculf has 4 dwellings of the Earldom which
   belong to (Upper) Penn, a manor of the Earl's; only one of them
   is habitable.

9 Henry of Ferrers has 1 unoccupied dwelling.

10 The priests of the Borough have 14.

*11 They all have full jurisdiction. The King has tax from them
   all each year.

12 Before 1066 the Borough of Stafford paid £9 of pence from
   all customary dues; two parts were the King's, the third
   the Earl's. Now King William has £7 from the Borough's payments,
   his part and the Earl's together. Robert has half the King's own
   part, by the King's gift, as he says.

.I.Rex Willelmvs.

.II.Eps de Ceftre.

.III.Abbatia Weftmonaſt.

.IIII Abbatia Bertonenſis.

.V.Æccła S Remigij Remſis.

.VI.Canonici de Stadford

7 de Handone.

.VII.Sanſon clericus.

.VIII.Comes Rogerius.

.IX.Hugo de Montgomeri.

.X.Henricus de Ferieres.

.XI.Robertus de Stadford.

.XII.Wilłs filius Anſculfi.

.XIII Ricardus foreſtarius.

.XIIII Rainald balgiole.

.XV.Radulf filius hubti.

.XVI.Nigellus

.XVII Chenuin 7 alij taini.

246 b

Terra Regis.　　*In Saisdon hvnd.*

Rex tenet *Svinesford*.Rex.E.tenuit.Ibi funt
:v.hidæ.Tra.ē.vi.car.In dnio.ē una 7 un feruus.

7 xiiii.uiłłi 7 iiii.bord.cū.vi.car.Ibi molin de.ii.fol.

7 iiii.ac p̃ti.Silua dimid leuū łg.7 iii.q̃rent lat.

Valet.lxx.ſolid.

Huic m̃ ptin dimid hida vafta in Cocretone.

Rex ten *Totehala*.Ibi.i.hida.Tra.ē.ii.car.Ibi funt
in dnio.7 iiii.uiłłi 7 iii.bord cū.i.car.Silua ibi dimid leuū
in long 7 lat.In Contone.ē.i.hida ptin ad Totehala.

T.R.E.uałb.xx.ſolid.Modo.xxx.ſolid.

In Wifteuuic.ē dimidia hida.7 ptin ad Totehala.Ibi
eft dimid car cū.i.uiłło.Valuit 7 uat.iiii.ſolid.

In *Billestvne* funt.ii.hidæ.Tra.ē.iiii.car.Ibi ſuȝ
viii.uiłłi 7 iii.bord cū.iii.car.Ibi.i.ac p̃ti.Silua
dimid leuū łg.7 dimid lat.Valuit.xx.fol.Modo.xxx.fol.

LIST OF LANDHOLDERS IN STAFFORDSHIRE

1	King William	9	Hugh of Montgomery
2	The Bishop of Chester	10	Henry of Ferrers
3	Westminster Abbey	11	Robert of Stafford
4	Burton Abbey	12	William son of Ansculf
5	St. Remy's Church, Rheims	13	Richard Forester
6	The Canons of Stafford	14	Reginald Balliol
*[7]	and of Wolverhampton	15	Ralph son of Hubert
	Samson the Clerk	16	Nigel
8	Earl Roger	17	Kenwin and other thanes.

1   LAND OF THE KING   246 b

In SEISDON Hundred

*1   The King holds (KING)SWINFORD. King Edward held it. 5 hides.
Land for 6 ploughs. In lordship 1; 1 slave;
    14 villagers and 4 smallholders with 6 ploughs.
    A mill at 2s; meadow, 4 acres; woodland ½ league long and
      3 furlongs wide.
Value 70s.
    To this manor belongs ½ hide, waste, in 'Crockington'.

2   The King holds TETTENHALL. 1 hide. Land for 2 ploughs. They
are there, in lordship.
    4 villagers and 3 smallholders with 1 plough.
    Woodland ½ league in length and width.
    In COMPTON, 1 hide which belongs to Tettenhall.
Value before 1066, 20s; now 30s.

3   In WIGHTWICK ½ hide; it belongs to Tettenhall.
    ½ plough with 1 villager.
The value was and is 4s.

4   In BILSTON 2 hides. Land for 4 ploughs.
    8 villagers and 3 smallholders with 3 ploughs.
    Meadow, 1 acre; woodland ½ league long and ½ wide.
The value was 20s; now 30s.

In *Bresmvndescote* . ē una caruc̅ træ uaſta.

Rex ten̄ *Wadnesberie* cū appendiciis.

Ibi . iii . hidæ . T̄ra . ē . ix . car̄ . In dn̄io . ē una . 7 un̄ ſeruus.

7 xvi . uilti 7 xi . borđ cū . vii . car̄ . Ibi molin̄ de . ii . ſot.

7 una ać p̄ti . Silua . ii . leuū l̄g . 7 una lat̄.

Blocheswic . ē mēbrū ejđ Maner̄ . Ibi Silua . iii . q̄rent̄

lonḡ . 7 una lat̄ . 7 In Scelfeld . ē hida uaſta . p̄tin̄ eiđ m̄.

Rex ten̄ *Pancriz* . Rex . E . tenuit.

Ibi . i . hida . T̄ra . ē . iiii . car̄ . In dn̄io ſunt . ii . 7 ii . ſerui.

7 ii . uilti 7 ii . borđ . cū . ii . car̄ . Ibi molin̄ de . v . ſoliđ . 7 xvi.

ać p̄ti . Silua hr̄ . i . leuū l̄g . 7 una lat̄ . Vat . xl . ſoliđ.

Ad hoc m̄ p̄tin̄ h̄ mēbra.

In *Tvrgarestone* . ē una hida . T̄ra . ē . iii . car̄

In *Draitone* . una hida uaſta . ē T̄ra . ē

In *Comegrave* . una hida . T̄ra . ē . iii . car̄.

In *Dvnestone* . ii . hidæ . T̄ra . ē . iiii . car̄.

In *Covelav* 7 *Beficote* . i . hida 7 dimiđ . T̄ra . ē . iii . car̄.

In dn̄io ſunt . ii . car̄ . 7 un̄ tain̄ . 7 ibi . xvi . uilti 7 xii . borđ

Int̄ om̄s hn̄t . vi . car̄ . 7 xviii . ać p̄ti . Silua dim̄ leuū l̄g . 7 iii.

q̄rent lat̄.

Tot̄ T.R.E . ualb̄ lxv . ſot . Modo . c . ſoliđ . *In Pirehel hđ*.

Rex ten̄ *Trenham* . Ibi . i . hida . T̄ra . ē . iii . car̄ . In dn̄io . ē

una . 7 v . uilt cū . i . borđ 7 p̄poſito hn̄t . iii . car̄ 7 dimiđ . Ibi

pb̄r 7 un̄ lib̄ ho̅ hn̄t . ii . car̄ . 7 iii . uilt 7 vi . borđ cū . i . car̄.

Silua ibi . i . leu l̄g . 7 dimiđ lat̄.

T.R.E . ualb̄ . c . ſoliđ . modo . cxv . ſoliđ.

[In OFFLOW Hundred]
5 In BESCOT 1 carucate of land, waste.

The King holds*
6 WEDNESBURY, with its dependencies. 3 hides. Land for 9 ploughs.
In lordship 1; 1 slave;
16 villagers and 11 smallholders with 7 ploughs.
A mill at 2s; meadow, 1 acre; woodland 2 leagues long
and 1 wide.
[Value...]
BLOXWICH is a member of this manor. Woodland 3 furlongs
long and 1 wide.
In SHELFIELD 1 hide, waste, which belongs to this manor.

[In CUTTLESTONE Hundred]
*7 PENKRIDGE. King Edward held it. 1 hide. Land for 4 ploughs.
In lordship 2; 2 slaves;
2 villagers and 2 smallholders with 2 ploughs.
A mill at 5s; meadow, 16 acres; woodland 1 league long
and 1 wide.
Value 40s.
These members belong to this manor....
in WOLGARSTON 1 hide. Land for 3 ploughs.
in DRAYTON 1 hide, waste. Land for....
in CONGREVE 1 hide. Land for 3 ploughs.
in DUNSTON 2 hides. Land for 4 ploughs.
in COWLEY and BEFFCOTE 1½ hides. Land for 3 ploughs.
In lordship 2 ploughs; 1 thane.
16 villagers and 12 smallholders have 6 ploughs between them.
Meadow, 18 acres; woodland ½ league long and 3 furlongs wide.
Total value before 1066, 65s; now 100s.

In PIREHILL Hundred
*8 TRENTHAM 1 hide. Land for 3 ploughs. In lordship 1;
5 villagers with 1 smallholder and a reeve have 3½ ploughs.
A priest and a free man have 2 ploughs; 3 villagers
and 6 smallholders with 1 plough.
Woodland 1 league long and ½ wide.
Value before 1066, 100s; now 115s.

Rex ten̄ *WIGETONE*. Ibi . ii . hidæ . Tra . ē . vi . cař . Ibi ſuÿ

viii . uiłłi 7 un̄ ſeru̇ 7 i . borđ . 7 iiii . burḡſes in Tamuuorde.

Int̄ om̄s hn̄t . vi . cař . Ibi . vi . q̊rent p̊ti in lonḡ . 7 ii . q̊ʒ lat̄.

Rex ten̄ *WINEHALA* . Ibi . iii . hidæ . Tra . ē . iiii . cař . Ibi ſunt

. v . uiłłi 7 iii . borđ cū . iii . cař . Ibi . i . ac̄ p̊ti . Valuit 7 uał xx . ſoliđ.

Rex ten̄ *ALREWAS* . Algar̄ tenuit . *IN OFFELAV HVND̄.*

Ibi ſunt . iii . hidæ . Tra ̇ē . viii . cař . In dn̄io ſunt . ii . 7 un̄ ſeruus.

7 xx . uiłłi 7 vi . borđ cū p̊bro hn̄t . vi . cař . Ibi xxiiii . ac̄ p̊ti.

Piſcař redđ mille q̊ngen̄t anguiłł . Silua . i . leuu̇ lḡ . 7 dim̄

lat̄ . T.R.E . ualḃ . x . liḃ . Modo ̇xi . liḃ.

Rex ten̄ *BROMELEI* . Herald̄ tenuit . Ibi ſunt . iii . hidæ.

Tra . ē . v . cař . In dn̄io ſunt . ii . cař . 7 ii . ſerui . 7 xi . uiłłi . 7 ii .

borđ cū . vi . cař . Ibi . xxv . ac̄ p̊ti . Silua . i . leuu̇ lḡ . 7 dim̄ lat̄.

Valuit 7 uał . c . ſoliđ.

Rex ten̄ *SCANDONE* . Algar̄ tenuit . cū append̄ ſuis . Ibi . i . hida.

Tra . ē . xv . cař . In dn̄io ſunt . ii . 7 xviii . uiłł 7 viii . borđ cū . viii . cař.

Ibi . viii . ac̄ p̊ti . Silua ht̄ . i . leuu̇ lḡ . 7 dimiđ lat̄.

T.R.E . ualḃ . c . ſoł . Modo ̇vi . liḃ.

246 c

Rex ten̄ *CERTELIE* . Algar̄ tenuit . Ibi . i . hida . Tra . ē

In dn̄io ſunt . ii . cař . 7 ix . uiłłi 7 vi . borđ cū . viii.

cař 7 dimiđ . Ibi . x . ac̄ p̊ti . Silua . i . leuu̇ lḡ . 7 dimiđ lat̄.

T.R.E . ualḃ . c . ſoliđ . Modo . x . ſoliđ plus.

Rex ten̄ *WLSTANETONE* . Algar̄ tenuit . Ibi . ii . hidæ cū

append̄ . Ibi . ii . cař in dn̄io . 7 xiiii . uiłłi 7 ii . borđ cū p̊bro

hn̄t . viii . cař . Silua . i . leuu̇ lḡ . 7 una q̊rent lat̄.

T.R.E . ualḃ . c . ſoliđ . Modo . vi . liḃ.

T.R.E. ualḃ
xxx . ſoł.
Modo . iiii . liḃ.

*[In OFFLOW Hundred]
*9 WIGGINGTON 2 hides. Land for 6 ploughs.
  8 villagers, 1 slave, 1 smallholder and 4 burgesses in Tamworth.
   They have 6 ploughs between them.
  Meadow 6 furlongs in length and 2 furlongs wide.
 Value before 1066, 30s; now £4.

10 WILLENHALL. 3 hides. Land for 4 ploughs.
  5 villagers and 3 smallholders with 3 ploughs.
  Meadow, 1 acre.
 The value was and is 20s.

 In OFFLOW Hundred
11 ALREWAS. Earl Algar held it. 3 hides. Land for 8 ploughs.
 In lordship 2; 1 slave.
  20 villagers and 6 smallholders with a priest have 6 ploughs.
  Meadow, 24 acres; a fishery which pays 1500 eels; woodland 1
   league long and ½ wide.
 Value before 1066 £10; now £11.

12 (KING'S) BROMLEY. Earl Harold held it. 3 hides. Land for 5 ploughs.
 In lordship 2 ploughs; 2 slaves;
  11 villagers and 2 smallholders with 6 ploughs.
  Meadow, 25 acres; woodland 1 league long and ½ wide.
 The value was and is 100s.

 [In PIREHILL Hundred]
13 SANDON. Earl Algar held it, with its dependencies. 1 hide.
 Land for 15 ploughs. In lordship 2;
  18 villagers and 8 smallholders with 8 ploughs.
  Meadow, 8 acres; woodland 1 league long and ½ wide.
 Value before 1066, 100s; now £6.

14 CHARTLEY. Earl Algar held it. 1 hide. Land for....   246 c
 In lordship 2 ploughs;
  9 villagers and 6 smallholders with 8½ ploughs.
  Meadow, 10 acres; woodland 1 league long and ½ wide.
 Value before 1066, 100s; now 10s more.

15 WOLSTANTON. Earl Algar held it. 2 hides, with its dependencies.
 In lordship 2 ploughs.
  14 villagers and 2 smallholders with a priest have 8 ploughs.
  Woodland 1 league long and 1 furlong wide.
 Value before 1066, 100s; now £6.

Rex ten̂ PINCHETEL . Algar tenuit . Ibi . ii . hidæ cū append̂.

Tra.ē.xi.car̂.In dn̄io funt.ii.7 xvii.uiłł 7 vi.bord̂ cū.viii.

car̂.Ib̂.ii.ac̄ p̂ti.Silua.i.leuu lḡ.7 ii.q̂rent̂ lat̄.Vał.vi.lib̂.

Rex ten̂ ROWECESTRE . Algar tenuit . Ibi.i.hida cū ap

pendiĉ Tra.ē.ix.car̂.In dn̄io funt.ii.7 xviii.uiłł

7 x.bord̂.cū.ix.car̂.Ibi molin̄ de.x.folid̂.7 xx.ac̄ p̂ti.

Silua.i.q̂rent̂ lḡ.7 tntd̂ lat̂

T.R.E.uałb̂.iiii.lib̂.Modo.viii.lib̂.

Rex ten̂ CRACHEMERS . Algar tenuit.Ibi dimid̂ hida

cū appendiĉ Tra.ē.vi.car̂.Ibi funt.ii.uiłłi 7 iiii.bord̂

cū.ii.car̂.7 vi.ac̄ p̂ti.Silua.i.leuu lḡ.7 tntd̂ lat̄.

Ibi molin̄ de.x.fot. Vał.x.folid̂.

Rex ten̂ WOTOCHESHEDE.Algar tenuit.Ibi dim̄ hida.

Tra.ē.x.car̂.In dn̄io funt.ii.cū.i.feruo.7 xxiiii.uiłł

7 xi.bord̂ cū.xi.car̂.Ibi.xvi.ac̄ p̂ti.Silua.ii.leuu lḡ.

7 totid̂ lat̂ T.R.E.uałb̂.vii.lib̂.Modo.viii.lib̂.

Rex ten̂ BERTONE . Algar tenuit.Ibi funt.iii.hidæ cū

append̂.Tra.ē.xviii.car̂.In dn̄io funt,ii.car̂.7 ii.ferui.

7 xvii.uiłł 7 viii.bord̂ cū.ix.car̂.Ibi.xx.ac̄ p̂ti.Silua

ht̄.ii.leuu lḡ.7 una lat̂.Ibi molin̄ de.vi.folid̂.

T.R.E.uałb̂.vi.lib̂.modo.vii.lib̂.

Rex ten̂ LEC.Algar tenuit.Ibi.i.hida.cū append̂

Tra.ē.xii.car̂.Ibi funt.xv.uiłłi 7 xiii.bord̂ cū.vi.

car̂.Ibi.iii.ac̄ p̂ti.Silua.iiii.leuu lḡ.7 totid̂ lat̂.

T.R.E.uałb̂.iiii.lib̂.modo.c.folid̂.

Rex ten̂ RVGELIE.Algar tenuit.Ibi.v.pars hidæ

Tra.ē.v.car̂.Ibi funt.ix.uiłłi cū.iii.car̂.7 molin̄ de

xxx.denar̂.7 iii.ac̄ p̂ti.Silua.iii.leuu lḡ.7 ii.lat̂.

T.R.E.uałb̂.xx.fot.Modo.xxx.folid̂.

16 PENKHULL. Earl Algar held it. 2 hides, with its dependencies.
    Land for 11 ploughs. In lordship 2;
        17 villagers and 6 smallholders with 8 ploughs.
        Meadow, 2 acres; woodland 1 league long and 2 furlongs wide.
        Value £6.

[In TOTMONSLOW Hundred]

17 ROCESTER. Earl Algar held it. 1 hide, with its dependencies.
    Land for 9 ploughs. In lordship 2;
        18 villagers and 10 smallholders with 9 ploughs.
        A mill at 10s; meadow, 20 acres; woodland 1 furlong long
          and as wide.
    Value before 1066 £4; now £8.

8 CRAKEMARSH. Earl Algar held it. ½ hide, with its dependencies.
    Land for 6 ploughs.
        2 villagers and 4 smallholders with 2 ploughs.
        Meadow, 6 acres; woodland 1 league long and as wide;
          a mill at 10s.
    Value 10s.

9 UTTOXETER. Earl Algar held it. ½ hide. Land for 10 ploughs.
    In lordship 2, with 1 slave;
        24 villagers and 11 smallholders with 11 ploughs.
        Meadow, 16 acres; woodland 2 leagues long and as wide.
    Value before 1066 £7; now £8.

[In OFFLOW Hundred]

0 BARTON (-under-Needwood). Earl Algar held it. 3 hides with its
    dependencies. Land for 18 ploughs. In lordship 2 ploughs; 2 slaves;
        17 villagers and 8 smallholders with 9 ploughs.
        Meadow, 20 acres; *woodland 2 leagues long and 1 wide;
          a mill at 6s.
    Value before 1066 £6; now £7.

[In TOTMONSLOW Hundred]

1 LEEK. Earl Algar held it. 1 hide, with its dependencies.
    Land for 12 ploughs.
        15 villagers and 13 smallholders with 6 ploughs.
        Meadow, 3 acres; woodland 4 leagues long and as wide.
    Value before 1066 £4; now 100s.

[In CUTTLESTONE Hundred]

2 RUGELEY. Earl Algar held it. The fifth part of 1 hide.
    Land for 5 ploughs.
        9 villagers with 3 ploughs.
        A mill at 30d; meadow, 3 acres; woodland 3 leagues long and 2 wide.
    Value before 1066, 20s; now 30s.

Rex ten̄ MEDEVELDE. Algar tenuit, Ibi. I. hida cū
appendic̄. Tra. e̅. xii. car̄. In dn̄io. e̅ una. 7 ix. uilti
7 iii. bord cū p̄bro hn̄t. iii. car̄. Ibi. viii. ac̄ p̄ti.
Silua. iiii. q̄rent lḡ. 7 ii. q̄rent lat̄.

T.R.E. ualb̄. xl. folid.

Rex ten̄ MERA. Algar tenuit. Ibi funt. iiii. hidæ cū append
Tra. e̅. x. car̄. In dn̄io. e̅ una. 7 ii. ferui. 7 xviii. uilti cū. x. car̄.
Ibi molin̄ de. iii. fot. 7 iiii. Mitt anguilt. Silua dim̄ leuū lḡ.
7 ii. q̄rent lat̄. T.R.E. ualb̄. iiii. lib̄. Modo. x. folid plus.

Rex ten̄ CHENET. Algar tenuit. Ibi. i. hida cū append.
Tra. e̅. xv. car̄. Ibi funt. viii. uilti 7 iii. bord cū. iii. car̄.
Silua. iiii. leuū lat̄. 7 vi. leuū lḡ. T.R.E. nil reddb̄. m̄ uat. xx. fot.

Rex ten̄ ELEFORD. Algar tenuit. Ibi funt. iii. hidæ. Tra. e̅
xi. car̄. In dn̄iq funt. iii. 7 xxiiii. uilti 7 viii. bord cū. viii. car̄.
Ibi. xxiiii. ac̄ p̄ti. 7 ii. molini de. xx. folid.

T.R.E. ualb̄. xi. lib̄. Modo. xii.

Rex ten̄ CHENEVARE. Algar tenuit. Ibi funt. v. hide 7 dim̄
cū append. Tra. e̅. xvi. car̄. In dn̄io. e̅ una. 7 iii. ferui. 7 xvii.
uilt 7 vii. bord cū p̄bro hn̄tes. x. car̄. Ibi. ii. molini de. xx. fot.
7 vi. ac̄ p̄ti. Silua. iii. leuū lḡ. 7 una lat̄. Valuit 7 uat. c. fot.

Rex ten̄ PATINGHA. Algar tenuit. Ibi funt. ii. hidæ. Tra. e̅. viii.
car̄. Ibi funt. iii. uilti cū p̄bro 7 x. bord hn̄tes. iii. car̄. Silua ibi
una leuū lḡ. 7 dimid leuū lat̄. Valuit 7 uat. iii. lib̄.

246 d

Rex ten̄ CLISTONE. Ibi. viii. hidæ funt cū append. Tra. e̅. iiii.
car̄. In dn̄io funt. ii. 7 ii. ferui. 7 xxx. iii. uilti 7 vii. bord cū p̄bro
hn̄t. xi. car̄. Ibi. ii. molini de. x. fot. 7 l. ac̄ p̄ti.

T.R.E. ualb̄. xi. lib̄. modo. xii. lib̄.

[In TOTMONSLOW Hundred]

3 MAYFIELD. Earl Algar held it. 1 hide, with its dependencies.
Land for 12 ploughs. In lordship 1,
9 villagers and 3 smallholders with a priest have 3 ploughs.
Meadow, 8 acres; woodland 4 furlongs long and 2 furlongs wide.
Value before 1066, 40s.

[In CUTTLESTONE Hundred]

4 MERE(TOWN). Earl Algar held it. 4 hides, with its dependencies.
Land for 10 ploughs. In lordship 1; 2 slaves;
18 villagers with 10 ploughs.
A mill at 3s; 4000 eels; woodland ½ league long and 2 furlongs wide.
Value before 1066 £4; now 10s more.

5 CANNOCK. Earl Algar held it. 1 hide, with its dependencies.
Land for 15 ploughs.
8 villagers and 3 smallholders with 3 ploughs.
Woodland (b) 4 leagues wide and (a) 6 leagues long.
Before 1066 it paid nothing; value now 20s.

[In OFFLOW Hundred]

6 ELFORD. Earl Algar held it. 3 hides. Land for 11 ploughs. In lordship 3;
24 villagers and 8 smallholders with 8 ploughs.
Meadow, 24 acres; 2 mills at 20s.
Value before 1066 £11; now [£] 12.

[In SEISDON Hundred]

7 KINVER. Earl Algar held it. 5½ hides, with its dependencies.
Land for 16 ploughs. In lordship 1; 3 slaves;
17 villagers and 7 smallholders with a priest who have 10 ploughs.
2 mills at 20s; meadow, 6 acres; woodland 3 leagues long and 1 wide.
The value was and is 100s.

8 PATTINGHAM. Earl Algar held it. 2 hides. Land for 8 ploughs.
3 villagers with a priest and 10 smallholders who have 3 ploughs.
Woodland 1 league long and ½ league wide.
The value was and is £3.

[In OFFLOW Hundred]

9 CLIFTON (CAMPVILLE). 8 hides, with its dependencies. 246 d
Land for 4 ploughs. In lordship 2; 2 slaves.
33 villagers and 7 smallholders with a priest have 11 ploughs.
2 mills at 10s; meadow, 50 acres.
Value before 1066 £11; now £12.

Rex ten̄ DRAITONE.Ibi.II.hidæ cū append̄.Tra.ē.IIII.car̄.
Ibi funt.IX.uitti 7 III.bord̄ cū.IIII.car̄ 7 dimid̄.7 VIII.burḡſes
in Tamuuorde huic ꝏ ꝑtin̄.7 ibi opant̄ ſic̄ alij uitti.
In ꝏ hꝗ rex.II.molin̄ de.XXI.ſot.7 XX.acſ ꝑti.Silua.II.leuū
lḡ.7 dimid̄ leuū lat̄.   Valuit 7 uat.IIII.lib̄.
Rex ten̄ OPEWAS.Ibi funt.III.hidæ.Tra.ē.VI.car̄.In dn̄io.ē
molin̄ de.XIII.ſolid̄ 7 IIII.den̄.7 XI.uitti 7 II.bord̄ cū.V.car̄.
Ibi.XXX.ac̄ ꝑti.Silua.VI.q̄rent̄.7 III.q̄ʒ lat̄.Valuit 7 uat XL.
Rex ten̄ HORVLVESTONE.Ibi funt.IIII.hidæ.   ⎰ ſolid̄.
Tra.ē.VIII.car̄.In dn̄io funt.ii.æ7 XVI.uitti 7 V.bord̄ hn̄t.IIII.
car̄.Ibi molin̄ de.IIII.ſot.7 ii.ſerui.Valuit 7 uat.VI.lib̄.
H.IIII.ꝏ or tenuit Algar comes.Sic̄ 7 ſupiores.

In BIDOLF.ē una hida cū append̄.Griſin tenuit.Tra.ē.III.car̄.
In BVCHENOLE tcia pars hidæ.Chetel tenuit.Tra.ē.III.car̄.
In ACLEI.una hida.Achi tenuit.Tra.ē.III.car̄.
In HEOLLA.ē dimid̄ v̄ træ Aluuard tenuit.Tra.ē.I.car̄.
In MESS   Vlfere tenuit.Tra.ē II.car̄.
In SCELFITONE.ē una v̄ træ.Aluiet tenuit.Tra.ē.II.car̄.
In HETONE.ē dimid̄ hida.Aluiet tenuit.Tra.ē.II.car̄.
In FVLEFORD.ē una v̄ træ.Almar tenuit.Tra.ē.II.car̄.
In MELEWICH.ē una v̄ træ.Rafuuin tenuit.Tra.ē.II.car̄.
In COTE.ē una v̄ træ cū append̄.Eluing tenuit.Tra.ē.I.car̄.
In HENTONE.ē una v̄ træ Vlfac tenuit.Tra.ē.II.car̄.
In HILDVLVESTVNE.ē dim v̄ træ.Vluric tenuit.Tra.ē dim car̄.
In COTEWOLDESTVNE.ē una v̄ træ.Rafuuin tenuer̄.Tra.ē.II.car̄.
In HELCOTE.ē dimid̄ v̄ træ.Turbern tenuit.Tra.ē.I.car̄.
In ESTONE.ē una car̄ træ 7 una v̄ træ.Oda tenuit.Tra.ē.I.car̄.

30 DRAYTON (BASSETT). 2 hides, with its dependencies. Land for 4 ploughs.
    9 villagers and 3 smallholders with 4½ ploughs;
       8 burgesses in Tamworth belong to this manor and work
       there like the other villagers.
    In the manor the King has 2 mills at 21s; meadow, 20 acres;
       woodland 2 leagues long and ½ league wide.
    The value was and is £4.

31 HOPWAS. 3 hides. Land for 6 ploughs. In lordship, a mill at 13s 4d;
    11 villagers and 2 smallholders with 5 ploughs.
    Meadow, 30 acres; woodland 6 furlongs [long] and 3 furlongs wide.
    The value was and is 40s.

32 HARLASTON. 4 hides. Land for 8 ploughs. In lordship 2.
    16 villagers and 5 smallholders have 4 ploughs.
    A mill at 4s; 2 slaves.
    The value was and is £6.
    Earl Algar held these 4 manors, as those above.

  In [PIREHILL] * Hundred, in*
33 BIDDULPH 1 hide, with its dependencies. Gruffydd held it.
    Land for 3 ploughs.

34 BUCKNALL the third part of a hide. Ketel held it.
    Land for 3 ploughs.

35 OAKLEY (in Mucklestone) 1 hide. Aki held it. Land for 3 ploughs.

36 HEIGHLEY ½ virgate of land. Alfward held it. Land for 1 plough.

37 (MILL)MEECE ...... Wulfhere held it. Land for 2 ploughs.

38 SHELTON 1 virgate of land. Alfgeat held it. Land for 2 ploughs.

39 HATTON ½ hide. Alfgeat held it. Land for 2 ploughs.

40 FULFORD 1 virgate of land. Aelmer held it. Land for 2 ploughs.

41 MILWICH 1 virgate of land. Rafwin held it. Land for 2 ploughs.

42 COTON (in Milwich) 1 virgate of land, with its dependencies.
    Ilving held it. Land for 1 plough.

43 ENSON 1 virgate of land. Wulfheah held it. Land for 2 ploughs.

44 HILDERSTONE ½ virgate of land. Wulfric held it. Land for ½ plough.

45 COTWALTON 1 virgate of land. Rafwin and Alwin held it.
    Land for 2 ploughs.

46 HILCOTE ½ virgate of land. Thorbern held it. Land for 1 plough.

47 ASTON (by-Stone) 1 carucate and 1 virgate of land. Oda held it.
    Land for 1 plough.

In _WODETONE_.ē tra.ɪɪ.car.Suain tenuit. _IN PEREOLLE HD._

In _STANTONE_.tra.ɪ.car. Archil tenuit.

In _MVSEDENE_ tra.ɪ.car.Vetred tenuit.

In _SCEON_   tra.ɪɪ.car. Aluuard tenuit.

In _STANESOPE_.tra.ɪ.car. Wodie tenuit.

In _FERNELEGE_.tra.ɪ.car. Aluuard tenuit.

In _ELVETONE_.tra.ɪɪ.car. Juuar tenuit.

In _DENESTONE_.tra.ɪɪ.car. Juuar tenuit

In _CVNESHALA_ træ una carucata. Vlfag tenuit.

In _CEDLA_ una car træ. Vlfag tenuit.

In _NIWETONE_.ɪɪ.car tre.Vluuiet tenuer. _Aluuard_

In _LVFAMESLES_.tra.ɪ.car. Vluuiet tenuit.

In _FOTESBROC_.tra.ɪ.car.Suuain tenuit.

In _ENEDVN_.tra.ɪ.car.Dunning tenuit.

In _RVGEHALA_ tra.ɪ.car. Wlmar tenuit.

In _RVDIERD_ tra.ɪ.car. Wlmar tenuit

In _RISETONE_.tra.ɪɪ.car.Vluiet tenuit.

Oīis ħ terra ʀᴇɢɪs Wafta eft

247 a

.II. **E**TERRA EPI DE CESTRE. _IN COLVESTAN HD._

Eᴘs De Cᴇsᴛʀᴇ teñ _BREVDE_. Æccła tenuit T.R.E.Ibi.v. hidæ.Tra.ē.xx.car.In dñio funt.ɪɪɪ.car.7 vɪɪɪ.ferui.7 xxɪɪɪɪ. uiłłi 7 xvɪɪɪ.borđ cū p̱ero hñt xɪɪɪɪ.car.Ibi.ɪɪ.molini de.ɪɪɪɪ. foliđ.7 ɪɪɪɪ.ać p̱ti.Silua.ɪ.leuū łg̃.7 dimiđ.7 una leuū łat. T.R.E.ualb̄.x.lib̄.Modo.c.foliđ.

In [TOTMONSLOW] * Hundred, in*

48 WOOTTON (under-Weaver) land for 2, or 3, ploughs. Swein held it.
49 STANTON land for 1 plough. Arkell held it.
50 MUSDEN land for 1 plough. Uhtred held it.
51 SHEEN land for 2, or 1, ploughs. Alfward held it.
52 STANSHOPE land for 1, or 2, ploughs. Wodi held it.
53 FARLEY land for 1, or 2, ploughs. Alfward held it.
54 ALTON land for 2 ploughs. Ivar held it.
55 DENSTONE land for 2 ploughs. Ivar held it.
56 CONSALL 1 carucate of land. Wulfheah held it.
57 CHEADLE 1 carucate of land. Wulfheah held it.
58 NEWTON 2 carucates of land. Wulfgeat and Alfward held it.
59 PAYNSLEY land for 1 plough. Wulfgeat held it.
60 FORSBROOK land for 1 plough. Swein held it.
61 ENDON land for 1, or 2, ploughs. Dunning held it.
62 ROWNALL land for 1 plough. Wulfmer held it.
63 RUDYARD land for 1, or 2, ploughs. Wulfmer held it.
64 RUSHTON land for 2 ploughs. Wulfgeat held it.
All this land of the King's is waste.

2   **LAND OF THE BISHOP OF CHESTER**   247 a

In CUTTLESTONE Hundred
1 The Bishop of Chester holds BREWOOD. The Church held it
   before 1066. 5 hides. Land for 20 ploughs.
   In lordship 3 ploughs; 8 slaves.
       24 villagers and 18 smallholders with a priest have 14 ploughs.
       2 mills at 4s; meadow, 4 acres; woodland 1½ leagues long
           and 1 league wide.
   Value before 1066 £10; now 100s.

Ipſe eṕs. teñ *BERCHESWIC*. Eccła tenuit T.R.E. Ibi . v ; hidæ
Tra.ē.iiii.caŕ. In dñio.ē una.7 ii.uiłłi cũ pƀro.
Ad hoc ꝏ ptiñ *WALETONE*. Ibi ſunt.iiii.borđ hñtes.ii.caŕ.7 ibi
.iiii.aĉ p̓ti. Silua.i.leuũ 7 dimiđ lḡ.7 una leuũ łat.
T.R.E.ualƀ . x . ſoł . modo . xv . ſoliđ.

r Ipſe eṕs teñ *ACTONE* 7 Roƀt de eo. Ibi   Tra.ē.iiii.caŕ
In dñio.ē una.7 x.uiłłi 7 viii.borđ cũ.iiii.caŕ. Ibi moliñ de.ii.
ſoliđ.7 viii.aĉ p̓ti. Silua.iii.q̃rent lḡ.7 ii.q̃ꝣ łat.
T.R.E.ualƀ.v.ſoł.Modo.xx.ſoliđ.   *IN PEREHOLLE HVND.*
Ipſe eṕs teñ *BROCTONE* 7 *BEDEHALA*. Ad Bercheſuuic ptiñ.7 ſuⱬ
Ipſe eṕs teñ *HAIWODE*. Sĉs *CEDDE* tenuit T.R.E.   ꝼ waſta.
Ibi dimiđ hida. Tra.ē.x.caŕ. In dñio ſunt.ĩi.7 ix.uiłłi 7 v.
borđ cũ pƀro hñt.vi.caŕ 7 dimiđ. Ibi moliñ de.v.ſoliđ.
Valuit 7 uał.xL.ſoliđ.   Hæ træ ſubſcriptæ ptiñ ad haiuuode.
q̇t træ Ipſe eṕs teñ *HVSTEDONE* 7 picot de eo.7 Nigełł de picot. Ibi
Ibi ſunt.v.uiłłi cũ.ii.caŕ.7 iii.aĉ p̓ti. Valuit 7 uał.x.ſoł 7 ix.deñ.
Ipſe eṕs teñ *VLSELEI*.7 Nigełł de eo. Ibi dĩ hida ptiñ ad
Haiuuode. Ibi ſunꞇ.iiii.uiłłi 7 ii.borđ cũ.i.caŕ.7 iii.aĉ p̓ti.
Valuit 7 uał . xL . denaŕ.

The Bishop himself holds*

2 BASWICH. The church held it before 1066. 5 hides. Land
for 4 ploughs. In lordship 1;
    2 villagers with a priest.
WALTON (-on-the-Hill) belongs to this manor.
    4 smallholders who have 2 ploughs.
    Meadow, 4 acres; woodland 1½ leagues long and 1 league wide.
Value before 1066, 10s; now 15s.

3 ACTON (TRUSSELL). Robert holds from him. [.... hides]
Land for 4 ploughs. In lordship 1;
    10 villagers and 8 smallholders with 4 ploughs.
    A mill at 2s; meadow, 8 acres; woodland 3 furlongs long
      and 2 furlongs wide.
Value before 1066, 5s; now 20s.

4 BROCTON and BEDNALL. They belong to Baswich and are waste.

In PIREHILL Hundred*
*5 (GREAT) HAYWOOD. St. Chad's held it before 1066. ½ hide.
Land for 10 ploughs. In lordship 2.
    9 villagers and 5 smallholders with a priest have 6½ ploughs.
    A mill at 5s.
The value was and is 40s.

The following lands belong to Haywood.

*6 HIXON. Picot holds from him, and Nigel from Picot. [....hides.]
    5 villagers with 2 ploughs.
    Meadow, 3 acres.
The value was and is 10s 9d.

7 WOLSELEY. Nigel holds from him. ½ hide, which belongs to Haywood.
    4 villagers and 2 smallholders with 1 plough.
    Meadow, 3 acres.
The value was and is 40d.

Ipſe eps̄ ten̄ FRODESWELLE.7 Ælfelm de eo.Ibi   p̄tin̄

ad Haiuuode.Tra.e.v.car̄.Ibi ſunt.iii.uilli 7 ii.borđ cū.ii.car̄.

Ibi.i.ac̄ p̄ti.Silua dimiđ leuū lḡ.7 ii.q̄ʒ lat̄.

T.R.E.ualb̄.iii.ſot.Modo.xiii.ſoliđ.7 iiii.denar̄.

In c̄o HAIWODA ſunt.vi.ac̄ p̄ti.Silua.ii.leuū lḡ.7 una lat̄.

Ipſe eps̄ ten̄ EGLESHELLE.Sc̄s CEDD tenuit IN PEREOLL HD̄.

Ibi.vii.hidæ ſunt.Tra.e̅   In dn̄io ſunt.iiii.car̄.7 ii.

ſerui.7 xiiii.uilli cū pb̄ro 7 ii.borđ hn̄t.vii.car̄.Ibi.iiii.ac̄

p̄ti.7 ii.molini de iiii.ſoliđ.   Vat.iiii.lib̄.

Ad hoc c̄o p̄tin̄ OFFELEIA.Leuenot ten̄ de ep̄o.

In dn̄io ht̄.|iii.car̄.7 iii.uilli 7 i.borđ cū.i.car̄.Ibi.i.ac̄ p̄ti.

Valuit 7 uat.x.ſoliđ. Ad EVND c̄o p̄tin̄ h̄ mēbra

In Fleteſbroc.tra.e̅.ii.car̄.In Ceruerneſt tra.e̅.i.car̄.

In Ceteruille tra.e̅.i.car̄.In Dorueſlau tra.e̅ dimiđ car̄.

In Cerueledone tra.e̅.ii.car̄.In Cerletone tra.e̅.i.car̄.

In Cota.tra.e̅.i.car̄.In MeSS.tra.e̅.ii.car̄.

In Badehale.tra.e̅ dim̄ car̄.In Slindone.tra.e̅.ii.car̄.

In Broc̄tone.tra.e̅.i.car̄. Om̄s hæ træ ſunt waſtæ.

In HEREBORGESTONE ht̄ eps̄ dim̄ car̄ træ.h̄ uaſta.e̅.

Ipſe eps̄ ht̄.iiii.uilt 7 iiii.borđ cū.ii.car̄ jn Haſpeleia

Ibi.e̅ tra.ii.car̄ 7 p̄tin̄ ad Ecleſhelle.Ibi.i.ac̄ p̄ti.Vat x.ſot.

In Crocheſtone.e̅ tra.iii.car̄.Ibi ht̄ eps̄.ii.uilt 7 viii.

borđ cū.ii.car̄.Ad Echeſelle p̄tin̄.Vat.xx.ſoliđ.

Ipſe eps̄ ten̄ EDELACHESTONE. IN TATESLAV HVND̄.

Sc̄s Cedd.tenuit T.R.E.Ibi.e̅ q̄rta pars uni hidæ.Tra

8 FRADSWELL. Alfhelm holds from him. [....hides]*, which belong to Haywood. Land for 5 ploughs.
     3 villagers and 2 smallholders with 2 ploughs.
     Meadow, 1 acre; woodland ½ league long and 2 furlongs wide.
Value before 1066, 3s; now 13s 4d.

9 In the manor of HAYWOOD, meadow, 6 acres; woodland 2 leagues long and 1 wide.

In PIREHILL Hundred

10 The Bishop holds ECCLESHALL himself. St. Chad's held it. 7 hides.
Land for....... In lordship 4 ploughs; 2 slaves.
     14 villagers with a priest and 2 smallholders have 7 ploughs.
     Meadow, 4 acres; 2 mills at 4s.
Value £4.

11 [BISHOPS]OFFLEY belongs to this manor. Leofnoth holds from the Bishop. In lordship he has land for 3 ploughs;
     3 villagers and 1 smallholder with 1 plough.
     Meadow, 1 acre.
The value was and is 10s.

These members belong to this manor : in*
FLASHBROOK land for 2 ploughs; CHARNES land for 1 plough;
CHATCULL land for 1 plough; 'DORSLOW' land for ½ plough; *
CHORLTON land for 2 ploughs; CHORLTON land for 1 plough;*
COTES land for 1 plough; (COLD)MEECE land for 2 ploughs;
BADEN HALL land for ½ plough; SLINDON land for 2 ploughs;
BROCKTON land for 1 plough. All these lands are waste.

12 In BROUGHTON the Bishop has ½ carucate of land. This is waste.

13 In ASPLEY the Bishop himself has
     4 villagers and 4 smallholders with 2 ploughs.
     Land for 2 ploughs; it belongs to Eccleshall.
     Meadow, 1 acre.
Value 10s.

14 In CROXTON land for 3 ploughs. The Bishop has
     2 villagers and 8 smallholders with 2 ploughs.
     It belongs to Eccleshall.
Value 20s.

The Bishop himself holds*
in TOTMONSLOW Hundred
15 ELLASTONE. St. Chad's held it before 1066. The fourth part of 1 hide.

ẽ.v.car.In dñio funt.ii.7 viii.uilli 7 v.bord cũ.iii.car.

Ibi.iii.ac ṗti.Silua.i.leuu lg.7 dimid lat.Val xii.fol.

T.R.E.ualb.ix.fol.   IN OFFELAV HVND.

Ipfe eṗs ten LECEFELLE.cũ appendic fuis.Ipfa æccła

tenuit.Ibi.xxv.hidæ|7 una v̄ træ.Tra.ẽ LXXIII.car.

In dñio funt.x.car.7 x.ferui.7 XLII.uilli 7 xii.bord

hñtes.xxi.car.7·ibi.v.canon hñt.iii.car.Ibi.xxx.v.ac

ṗti.7 ii.molini de.iiii.folid. ' Valuit 7 ual.xv.lib.

Ad hoc ꝏ ptin h̄ mẽbra.Padintone.tra.iiii.car.

247 b

7 duæ Humeruuich.træ.v.carucatæ.7 Tichebroc

tra.i.car.7 Nortone 7 Wereleia.iiii.caruc træ.

7 Rouueleia.i.caruc træ.Hæ træ oms funt waftæ.

Ipfe eṗs ten SCOTESLEI.7 Nigell de eo.Ibi.ii.car træ.In dñio

ẽ una.7 viii.uilli 7 ii.bord cũ.i.car.Ibi.i.ac ṗti.Val.x.folid.

Ipfe eṗs ten MORTONE.7 Nigell de eo.Ibi.ii.car træ.In dñio

ẽ una car.7 ii.uilt 7 iiii.bord cũ dim car.Ibi.ii.ac ṗti.Val.v.fol.

Ipfe eṗs ten DREGETONE 7 Nigell de eo.

Ibi.ẽ un uilts cũ dimid car. Valuit 7 ual.xxx.denar.

Ipfe eṗs ten SOTEHELLE.7 Frane 7 Fragrin de eo.Tra.ẽ.ii.

car.Ibi funt.iii.uilli.7 i.feru.7 vi.bord cũ.iii.car.Ibi.iii.

ac ṗti.Valuit 7 ual.x.folid.H Mẽbra ptin ad eund ꝏ.

In Bramelie 7 Podemore tra.ẽ.iii.car.In Tuneftal tra.ii.car.

In Suefnefhed tra.ẽ.iiii.car.In Linehalle tra.ẽ.iii.car.

In Waletone tra.ẽ.iiii.car.In Edboldeftone tra.ẽ.ii.car.

In Wodeftone tra.ẽ.iii.car.In Chniteftone.tra.ẽ.ii.car.

Land for 5 ploughs. In lordship 2;
   8 villagers and 5 smallholders with 3 ploughs.
   Meadow, 3 acres; woodland 1 league long and ½ wide.
Value 12s; before 1066, 9s.

in OFFLOW Hundred

6 LICHFIELD, with its dependencies. The church held it itself. 25½ hides
and 1 virgate of land. Land for 73 ploughs.
In lordship 10 ploughs; 10 slaves;
   42 villagers and 12 smallholders who have 21 ploughs.
     5 canons have 3 ploughs.
   Meadow, 35 acres; 2 mills at 4s.
The value was and is £15.
These members belong to this manor: PACKINGTON, land for 4 ploughs;
the two HAMMERWICHES, 5 carucates of land; STYTCHBROOK, land 247 b
for 1 plough; NORTON (CANES) and WYRLEY 4 carucates of land;
ROWLEY, 1 carucate of land. All these lands are waste.

[in PIREHILL Hundred]
17 COLEY. Nigel holds from him. 2 carucates of land. In lordship 1 plough;
   8 villagers and 2 smallholders with 1 plough.
   Meadow, 1 acre.
Value 10s.

18 MORETON (in Colwich). Nigel holds from him. 2 carucates of land.
In lordship 1 plough;
   2 villagers and 4 smallholders with ½ plough.
   Meadow, 2 acres.
Value 5s.

19 DROINTON. Nigel holds from him.
   1 villager with ½ plough.
The value was and is 30d.

20 SUGNALL. Fran and Fragrin hold from him. Land for 2 ploughs.
   3 villagers, 1 slave and 6 smallholders with 3 ploughs.
   Meadow, 3 acres.
The value was and is 10s.
These members belong to this manor: in (GERARD'S) BROMLEY and
PODMORE land for 3 ploughs; TUNSTALL land for 2 ploughs.
SWYNCHURCH land for 4 ploughs; ELLENHALL land for 3 ploughs;
*WALTON land for 4 ploughs; ADBASTON land for 2 ploughs;
WOOTTON land for 3 ploughs; KNIGHTON land for 2 ploughs.

Has.viii.bereuu ten.iiii.teini.7 iiii.francig.7 alii hões de eis.
Ibi funt in dñio.iii.car.7 xiiii.uilli.7 xxxiiii.bord hñtes
.x.car.jnt oms 7 xii.ač pti.

Tot T.R.E ualb.lx.ii.folid.Modo fimilit int oms.

Ipfe eps ten CESTEFORDE.tra ibi.iii.car.7 Eftone 7 dochefig
Ibi tra.iii.car.7 Brigeford.Ibi tra.ii.car.7 Cote.Ibi tra.ii.bou.
Has tras ten.ii.francig 7 un tein de epo.Ad Eclefhelle ptin.
Ibi funt.x.uilli 7 vi.bord cu.v.car.7 hñt.v.ačs pti.
Silua huj ꝏ Eclefhelle ht.iiii.leuu lg.7 ii.leuu lat.
Ipfe eps ten LICEFELLE.7 ja retro defcript eft.Ibi ptin
Silua.viii.leuu 7 dim 7 vii.ꝗrent lg.7 vi.leuu 7 dimid
7 viii.ꝗrent lat. Ad ipfu ꝏ ptin h mebra.
Hortone.tra.ii.car.Aluuin ten.ꝼPagintone.tra.iiii.car.
Vlchetel ten.ꝼTamahore tra.iiii.car.Nigell ten.
ꝼHadefacre tra.v.car.Robt ten.ꝼHintes tra.vii.car.
Ofuuold ten.ꝼLochefhale tra.iiii.car.Rauen 7 Aluuin ten.
ꝼRiduuare tra.i.car.Alric ten.ꝼWeforde 7 Buroueftone
7 Litelbech tra.iiii.car.Radulf ten.ꝼFraiforde tra
vi.car.Rannulf ten.ꝼTimmor tra.i.car.Rannulf ten.
ꝼHoreborne tra.i.car.Robt ten.ꝼSmedeuuich.tra
ii.car.ꝼTibintone tra.v.car.Wills ten.
In his tris uel Bereuu funt in dñio.vii.car.7 lx.uilli
7 xxii.bord cu.xxv.car.Int oms.lii.ač pti.7 Molin.
Valentia in ꝏ eft cõputata.

247 c

.III. TERRA SĈI PETRI WESTMONAST.

ABBATIA ş PETRI Weftmonast ten PERTONE.Ibi
.iii.hidæ.Tra.ē.vi.car.In dñio.ē una.7 xiii.uilli 7 ii.bord
7 un lib hõ cu.v.car.Ibi.viii.ač pti.Silua dimid leuu
lg.7 tntd lat.   Valuit 7 ual.xl.folid.

4 thanes and 4 Frenchmen hold these 8 outliers, and other men
from them. In lordship 3 ploughs;
    14 villagers and 34 smallholders who have 10 ploughs between them.
    Meadow, 12 acres.
Total value before 1066, 62s; now the same, between them all.

21 SEIGHFORD. Land for 3 ploughs. ASTON AND DOXEY. Land for 3 ploughs.
BRIDGEFORD. Land for 2 ploughs. COTON (CLANFORD).Land for 2 oxen.
2 Frenchmen and 1 thane hold these lands from the Bishop.
They belong to Eccleshall.
    10 villagers and 6 smallholders with 5 ploughs. They have
    meadow, 5 acres. The woodland of this manor, Eccleshall, has
        4 leagues length and 2 leagues width.

22 LICHFIELD. It has already been described before .
    A woodland, 8½ leagues and 7 furlongs long and 6½ leagues
    and 8 furlongs wide, belongs there.
These members belong to this manor:
'HORTON', land for 2 ploughs; Alwin holds it. PACKINGTON, land
for 4 ploughs; Ulfketel holds it. TAMHORN, land for 4 ploughs;
Nigel holds it. HANDSACRE, land for 5 ploughs; Robert holds it.
HINTS, land for 7 ploughs; Oswald holds it. YOXALL land for 4 ploughs;
Rafwin and Alwin hold it. (PIPE) RIDWARE land for 1 plough.
Alric holds it. WEEFORD, 'BURWESTON' and 'LITTLEBEECH', land for 4 ploughs,
Ralph holds it. FREEFORD, land for 6 ploughs; Ranulf holds it.
'TYMMORE', land for 1 plough; Ranulf holds it. HARBORNE*, land
for 1 plough; Robert holds it. SMETHWICK, land for 2 ploughs.
TIPTON land for 5 ploughs; William holds it.*
In these lands or outliers, 7 ploughs in lordship;
    60 villagers and 22 smallholders with 25 ploughs. Between them all,
    meadow, 52 acres; a mill.
The valuation is accounted for in the manor.

3   LAND OF ST. PETER'S OF WESTMINSTER   247 c

[In SEISDON Hundred]
1 The Abbey of St. Peter's of Westminster holds PERTON. 3 hides.
    Land for 6 ploughs. In lordship 1;
        13 villagers, 2 smallholders and 1 free man with 5 ploughs.
        Meadow, 8 acres; woodland ½ league long and as wide.
    The value was and is 40s.

.IIII. TERRA SCÆ MARIÆ DE BERTONE.

ABBATIA s̄ MARIÆ de Bertone teñ in uilla Stadford
unā hid 7 dimid. Tra.ē.II.car. Ibi funt in dñio.7 IX.uilli
hūt ibi.II.car. Ibi.XVI.ac̄ pti. Silua dimid leuu lḡ.
7 tñtd lat.   T.R.E.ualb̄ LX.fot.Modo.LXX.folid.
Ipfa abbatia teñ BRANTESTONE.Godeua tenuit T.R.E.
Ibi.ē.I.hida 7 dimid.Tra.ē.v.car̄.In dñio.ē una 7 dim.
7 v.uilli 7 III.bord cū.III.car̄. Ibi.XXIIII.ac̄ pti.Silua
dimid leuu lḡ.7 tñtd lat.   Valuit.LX.fot.Modo.XL.fot.
Ipfa abbatia teñ WITMERE.Ibi.I.hida 7 dim cū append
fuis.Tra.ē.VII.car̄.In dñio funt.II.7 VI.uilli hūt.II.
car̄.Ibi.IIII.ac̄ pti.Silua|leuu lḡ.7 alia lat.
T.R.E.ualb̄.IIII.lib̄.7 poſt.XX.fot.Modo.L.fot.
Ipfa abbatia teñ STRATONE.Ibi.I.hida 7 dimid.Tra.ē.II.
car̄.In dñio.ē una.7 VIII.uilli 7 II.bord hūt.v.car̄.Ibi
XXVIII.ac̄ pti.
T.R.E.ualb̄.LX.fot.7 poſt.XX.folid.Modo.XL.folid.
Ipfa abbatia teñ BRVNLEGE.Ibi dimid hida cū append.
Tra.ē.I.car̄.Ipfa.ē in dñio.7 pbr cū.I.uillo 7 uno bord
hūt.I.car̄.Silua ibi.II.leuu lḡ.7 una lat.
Valuit.X.folid.Modo.xx.fot.
Ipfa abbatia teñ DERLAVESTONE.7 duo hōēs de ea.Ibi.III.
virg træ.Tra.ē.II.car̄.Ibi funt.II.uilli
Ibi.VI.ac̄ pti.Silua.II.qrent lḡ.7 una qrent lat.
T.R.E.ualb̄.XXX.folid.7 poſt.X.fot.Modo.XXVII.fot.7 II.den.

[In OFFLOW Hundred]
The Abbey of St. Mary's of Burton holds 1½ hides in the town of
STAFFORD*. Land for 2 ploughs. They are there, in lordship.
9 villagers have 2 ploughs.
Meadow, 16 acres; woodland ½ league long and as wide.
Value before 1066, 60s; now 70s.

The Abbey itself holds*
2 BRANSTON. Countess Godiva held it before 1066. 1½ hides.
Land for 5 ploughs. In lordship 1½ ploughs;
5 villagers and 3 smallholders with 3 ploughs.
Meadow, 24 acres; woodland ½ league long and as wide.
The value was 60s; now 40s.

3 WETMORE. 1½ hides with its dependencies. Land for 7 ploughs.
In lordship 2.
6 villagers have 2 ploughs.
Meadow, 4 acres; woodland 1 league long and another wide.
Value before 1066 £4; later 20s; now 50s.

4 STRETTON. 1½ hides. Land for 2 ploughs. In lordship 1.
8 villagers and 2 smallholders have 5 ploughs.
Meadow, 28 acres.
Value before 1066, 60s; later 20s; now 40s.

5 (ABBOTS) BROMLEY. ½ hide with its dependencies.
Land for 1 plough. It is in lordship.
A priest with 1 villager and 1 smallholder have 1 plough.
Woodland 2 leagues long and 1 wide.
The value was 10s; now 20s.

6 DARLASTON. 2 men hold from the Abbey. 3 virgates of land.
Land for 2 ploughs.
2 villagers.
Meadow, 6 acres; woodland 2 furlongs long and 1 furlong wide.
Value before 1066, 30s; later 10s; now 27s 4d.

Ipſa abbatia ten̄ *LEGE*.Ibi.iii.virḡ træ . T̄ra.ē.iii.car̄.

In dn̄io.ē una.Ibi un̄ lib̄ hō 7 x.uiłłi hn̄tes.v.car̄.

Silua ibi.i.leuū łḡ.7 tn̄td̄ lat̄.　　　　Valuit 7 uał.xl.ſolid̄.

Ipſa abbatia ten̄ *ACOVRE*.Ibi.iii.v træ cū append ſuis.

T̄ra.ē.ii.car̄.Eddulf ten̄ ad censū.Ibi.ē un̄ moliñ.

Silua dimid̄ leuū łḡ.7 iii.q̄rent lat̄.　　　　Vał.xx.ſoł.

Ipſa abbatia ten̄ *WITESTONE*.7 Nauuen de ea.Ibi.i.hida.

T̄ra.ē.i.car̄.Ibi.ē ipſa cū.i.uiłło 7 ii.bord.Vał.iiii.ſoł.

Ipſa abbatia ten̄ *BEDDINTONE*.Ibi dimid̄ hida.

T̄ra.ē.ii.car̄.Ibi.ē un̄ uiłłs.

Silua dimid̄ leuū łḡ.7 tn̄td̄ lat̄.Valuit.xiii.ſoł.m̄.vii.ſoł

7 iiii.denar̄.

.V. 　　　TERRA SC̄I REMIGIJ. *IN PIREHOLLE HD̄.*

E̢ccla s̄ REMIGIJ ten̄.dimid̄.hid̄ in *MEPFORD*.7 Nauuen

ten̄ de æccła.T̄ra.ē.ii.car̄.In dn̄io.ē una.7 iiii.uiłłi 7 iii.

bord̄ cū.ii.car̄.Ibi.iii.ac̄ p̄ti.Silua.iii.q̄rent łḡ.7 una lat̄.

Valet.xiii.ſolid̄.　　　　*IN OFFELAV HVND̄.*

Ipſa æccła ten̄ in *RIDEWARE*.i.v træ.T̄ra.ē.i.car̄.Godric

ten̄ de æccła.Ibi ht̄ dim̄ car̄.7 ii.uiłłi dimid̄.Ibi moliñ de.ii.

ſolid̄.7 ii.ac̄ p̄ti.Valet.v.ſolid̄.

Has.ii.tras ded̄ Algar S̄ Remigio.

247 d

.VI. In *STATFORD* Ciuitate ht̄ rex.xiii.canonicos p̄benda

rios.7 ten̄.iii.hid̄ de rege in elemoſina.T̄ra.ē.ix.car̄.

Ibi ſunt.iiii.uiłłi 7 viii.bord̄ 7 iiii.ſerui.hn̄tes.ii.car̄.

Ibi moliñ de.iiii.ſolid̄.7 ii.q̄rent p̄ti in łḡ.7 una q̄z lat̄.

Valuit.xx.ſoł.T.R.E.modo.lx.ſolid̄.

[In TOTMONSLOW Hundred]

7 LEIGH. 3 virgates of land. Land for 3 ploughs. In lordship 1.
   1 free man and 10 villagers who have 5 ploughs.
   Woodland 1 league long and as wide.
   The value was and is 40s.

8 OKEOVER. 3 virgates of land with its dependencies.
   Land for 2 ploughs. Edwulf holds it, at dues.
   A mill; woodland ½ league long and 3 furlongs wide.
   Value 20s.

[In CUTTLESTONE Hundred]

9 WHISTON. Nawen holds from the Abbey. 1 hide. Land for 1 plough.
   It is there, with
   1 villager and 2 smallholders.
   Value 4s.

0 PILLATON. ½ hide. Land for 2 ploughs.
   1 villager.
   Woodland ½ league long and as wide.
   The value was 13s; now 7s 4d.

5   LAND OF ST. REMY'S (CHURCH)

In PIREHILL Hundred

1 St. Remy's Church holds ½ hide in MEAFORD. Nawen holds
   from the Church. Land for 2 ploughs. In lordship 1;
   4 villagers and 3 smallholders with 2 ploughs.
   Meadow, 3 acres; woodland 3 furlongs long and 1 wide.
   Value 13s.

In OFFLOW Hundred

2 The Church holds 1 virgate of land itself in (HAMSTALL) RIDWARE.
   Land for 1 plough. Godric holds it from the Church. He has ½ plough.
   2 villagers [have] ½ (plough).
   A mill at 2s; meadow, 2 acres.
   Value 5s.
   Earl Algar gave these two lands to St. Remy's.

6   [THE CANONS OF STAFFORD]   247 d

[In PIREHILL Hundred]

1 In the City of STAFFORD the King has 13 prebendary canons.
   They hold 3 hides from the King in alms. Land for 9 ploughs.
   4 villagers, 8 smallholders and 4 slaves who have 2 ploughs.
   A mill at 4s; meadow 2 furlongs in length and 1 furlong wide.
   Value before 1066, 20s; now 60s.

.VII. CTERRA CLERICOʒ DE HANDONE.

Cᴀɴᴏɴɪcɪ de ʜᴀɴᴛᴏɴᴇ teñ . ɪ . hidā de Sanſone . Tra̅ . e̅ . ɪɪɪ .
ca̅r . T.R.E. fue̅r ibi . vɪɪɪ . ca̅r . modo ſunt . x . 7 xɪɪɪɪ . ſerui . 7 vɪ .
uiłłi 7 xxx . bord cu̅ . ɪx . ca̅r . Ibi . ɪɪ . a̅c p̅ti .

Ipſi canoñ teñ in Eʀɴʟᴇɢᴇ . ɪɪ . hid̅ . Tra̅ . e̅ . vɪ . ca̅r . In dn̅io . e̅ una
ca̅r . 7 ɪɪ . ſerui . 7 vɪɪ . uiłłi 7 ɪɪɪ . bord cu̅ . ɪɪɪɪ . ca̅r . Ibi . ɪɪɪ . lib̅i ho̅es .
Silua . vɪ . q̇rent lg̅ . 7 ɪɪɪɪ . q̇rent lat̅ .

Ad hanc tra̅ p̅tiñ dimid̅ hida in alia Ernlege . qua̅ Osb̅ñ . f . Ricardi
ui tollit canoñ . Tra̅ . e̅ . ɪ . ca̅r . Ibi . e̅ cu̅ . ɪɪɪɪ . uiłłis . Vał . x . ſolid̅ .

In Bɪscᴏᴘᴇsʙᴇʀɪᴇ hn̅t ipſi canoñ . ɪ . virg tra̅ . Tra̅ . e̅ dimid̅ ca̅r .
Ibi . e̅ uñ lib̅ ho̅ cu̅ . ɪ . ca̅r . Vał . xɪɪ . deñ .

In Cᴏᴛᴇ hn̅t . ɪ . virg tra̅ . Tra̅ . e̅ dimid̅ ca̅r . Hanc h̅t ibi uñ lib̅
ho̅ . 7 uał . xɪɪ . denar .

In Tᴏᴛᴇɴʜᴀʟᴇ hn̅t . ɪ . hida̅ . Tra̅ . e̅ . ɪɪ . ca̅r 7 dimid̅ . 7 ibi ſuꝷ . ɪɪɪ .
ca̅r . cu̅ . ɪ . uiłło 7 ɪɪɪ . bord̅ .

H̅ tra̅ n̅ p̅tiñ ad Hantone . ſed̅ . e̅ elemoſina regis ad eccłam ejd̅ uillæ .

De ead̅ elemoſina hn̅t p̅bri de Totenhale . ɪ . hid̅ in Bɪʟʀᴇʙʀᴏcʜ .
Ibi ſunt . ɪɪ . lib̅i ho̅es cu̅ . ɪ . uiłło 7 ɪɪ . bord̅ . hn̅tes . ɪɪ . ca̅r 7 dimid̅ .

Ipſi canoñ hn̅t in ʜᴀsᴡɪc . v . hid̅ . Tra̅ . e̅ . vɪɪɪ . ca̅r . Modo . e̅
waſta ꝑpt foreſta̅ regis . Ibi p̅tinuit medietas ſiluæ . quæ . e̅ in foreſta .

Ipſi canoñ hn̅t . v . hid̅ in Wᴏᴅɴᴇsꜰᴇʟᴅᴇ . Tra̅ . e̅ . ɪɪɪ . ca̅r .
Ibi ſunt . vɪ . uiłłi 7 vɪ . bord̅ hn̅tes . vɪ . ca̅r .
Silua paſtilis dimid̅ leuu̅ lg̅ . 7 ɪɪɪ . q̇rent lat̅ .

7   *LAND OF THE CLERGY OF WOLVERHAMPTON

[In SEISDON Hundred]

1 The Canons of WOLVERHAMPTON hold 1 hide from Samson.*
   Land for 3 ploughs. Before 1066, 8 ploughs; now 10; 14 slaves.
     6 villagers and 30 smallholders with 9 ploughs.
     Meadow, 2 acres.

2 The Canons hold 2 hides themselves in (UPPER) ARLEY.
   Land for 6 ploughs. In lordship 1 plough; 2 slaves;
     7 villagers and 3 smallholders with 4 ploughs; 3 free men.
     Woodland 6 furlongs long and 4 furlongs wide.
   To this land belongs ½ hide in the other Arley which Osbern
   son of Richard took from the Canons by force. Land for 1 plough.
   It is there with
     4 villagers.
   Value 10s.

3 In BUSHBURY the Canons have 1 virgate of land themselves.
   Land for ½ plough.
     1 free man with 1 plough.
   Value 12d.

4 In (TRES)COTT they have 1 virgate of land. Land for ½ plough.
     1 free man has it there.
   Value 12d.

5 In TETTENHALL they have 1 hide. Land for 2½ ploughs. 3 ploughs
   there, with
     1 villager and 3 smallholders.
   This land does not belong to Wolverhampton, but is the King's
   alms to the Church of this town. From the same alms the
   priests of Tettenhall have 1 hide in BILBROOK.
     2 free men with 1 villager and 2 smallholders who have 2½ ploughs.

6 The Canons have 5 hides themselves in ASHWOOD (?).
   Land for 8 ploughs; now waste, because of the King's Forest.
   Half of the woodland in the Forest belonged there.

[In OFFLOW Hundred]

7 The Canons have 5 hides themselves in WEDNESFIELD.
   Land for 3 ploughs.
     6 villagers and 6 smallholders who have 6 ploughs.
     Woodland pasture ½ league long and 3 furlongs wide.

Ipſi canon̄ ten̄ . ıı . hiđ in *WINENHALE* . Tra . ē . ı . car̄.

Ibi ſunt . ııı . uiłłi ꝫ v . borđ hn̄tes . ııı . car̄.

Ipſi ten̄ dimiđ hiđā in *PELESHALE* . Tra . ē . ı . car̄ . h̄ uaſta . ē.

Ipſi ten̄ . ııı . virg̃ træ in *ILTONE* . Tra . ē . ı . car̄ . Ibi . ıı . liƀi hões

ꝫ ıııı . borđ hn̄t . ıı . car̄ . In *HOCINTVNE* . ı . hiđ . waſta.

Tota h̄ canonicoꝫ tra . ualet p̃ an̄n̄ . vı . liƀ.

IN COLVESTAN HD.

Eduin ꝫ Alric
Sanson ten̄ de rege . ꝫ p̃ƀri de eo . ııı . hiđ træ in *HARGEDONE*.

Tra . ē . ıı . car̄ . In dn̄io . ē una . ꝫ un̄ ſeru . Ibi . ı . miles ꝫ ııı . uiłłi

cū . vıı . borđ hn̄t . ııı . car̄ . Silua ibi dimiđ leuū l̄g . ꝫ ıııı . q̃ꝫ lat̄.

Valuit . ıı . ſoł . Modo . x . ſoliđ.

Ipſi ten̄ . ı . hiđā in *CHENWARDESTONE* . Tra . ē . ı . car̄ . In dn̄io

ſunt . ıı . car̄ . ꝫ ııı . ſerui . ꝫ ııı . borđ . Ibi moliñ de . ııı . ſoliđ.

ꝫ vııı . ac̄ p̃ti .   T.R.E . ualƀ . xıı . den̄ . modo uał . x . ſoliđ.

Has . ıı . tras tenuit s̄ MARIA dē hantone . T.R.E.

Ipſi ten̄ . ıı . hiđ in *HALTONE* Tra . ē . ıı . car̄ . In dn̄io . ē una.

cū . ı . ſeruo . ꝫ un̄ lıƀ hō cū . ıı . borđ hē car̄ ꝫ dimiđ . ꝫ ııı . uiłłi

hn̄t ibi . ı . car̄ .   Valuit . xıı . den̄ . Modo . x . ſoliđ.

Ipſi hn̄t in *FERDESTAN* . ı . hiđā waſtā . IN COLVESTAN HD.

de Rege
In *PANCRIZ* ten̄ . ıx . clerici . ı . hiđ . Tra . ē . ıııı . car̄ . In dn̄io

ſunt . v . car̄ . ꝫ vı . ſerui . ꝫ vıı . uiłłi cū . ııı . car̄.

Valuit . ııı . ſoł . Modo . x . ſoliđ.

Ipſi clerici ten̄ . ıı . hiđ ꝫ ııı . virg̃ træ in *GENESHALE* . Tra . ē

ıı . car̄ . In dn̄io ſunt . ıııı . car̄ . ꝫ vııı . uiłłi ꝫ ıııı . borđ cū . ıı.

car̄ . Ibi moliñ de . xıı . den̄ .   Valuit . ıı . ſoł . Modo . xv . ſoł.

8 The Canons hold 2 hides themselves in WILLENHALL. Land for 1 plough.
   3 villagers and 5 smallholders who have 3 ploughs.
9 They hold ½ hide themselves in PELSALL. Land for 1 plough. Waste.
10 They hold 3 virgates of land themselves in HILTON. Land for 1 plough.
   2 free men and 4 smallholders have 2 ploughs.
11 In OGLEY HAY, 1 hide waste.
12 Total annual value of this land of the Canons £6.

In CUTTLESTONE Hundred
13 Samson holds 3 hides of land in HATHERTON from the King.
   The priests Edwin and Alric hold from him. Land for 2 ploughs.
   In lordship 1; 1 slave.
       1 man-at-arms and 3 villagers with 7 smallholders have
           3 ploughs.
   Woodland ½ league long and 4 furlongs wide.
   The value was 2s; now 10s.

14 They hold 1 hide themselves in KINVASTON. Land for 1 plough.
   In lordship 2 ploughs; 3 slaves;
       3 smallholders.
   A mill at 3s; meadow, 8 acres.
   Value before 1066, 12d; now 10s.
       St. Mary's of Wolverhampton held these two lands before 1066.

15 They hold 2 hides themselves in HILTON. Land for 2 ploughs.
   In lordship 1, with 1 slave.
       1 free man with 2 smallholders has 1½ ploughs.
       3 villagers have 1 plough.
   The value was 12d; now 10s.

In CUTTLESTONE Hundred*
16 They have 1 hide themselves in FEATHERSTONE. Waste.

17 In PENKRIDGE 9 clerics hold 1 hide from the King.
   Land for 4 ploughs. In lordship 5 ploughs; 6 slaves;
       7 villagers with 3 ploughs.
   The value was 3s; now 10s.

18 In GNOSALL the clerics hold 2 hides and 3 virgates of land themselves.
   Land for 2 ploughs. In lordship 4 ploughs;
       8 villagers and 4 smallholders with 2 ploughs.
   A mill at 12d.
   The value was 2s; now 15s.

.VIII CTERRA COMITIS ROGERIJ.

COMES Rogerius teñ *CLAVERLEGE* . Ibi funt . xx . hidæ
Algar tenuit . Tra . ē . xxxii . car . In dñio funt . v . car.

7 xxxii . uilli 7 xiii . borđ hñtes . xxiii . car . Ibi molinũ
de . v . foliđ . 7 xii . ač p̃ti . Silua . ii . leuu lg̃ . 7 dim leuu
lat . T.R.E. ualb . vii . lib 7 x . foliđ . Modo . x . lib.

Ipfe com teñ *NORDLEGE* . Algar tenuit . Ibi funt . ii . hidæ.
Tra . ē . xii . car . In dñio funt . iii . car . 7 vii . uilli 7 ii . borđ
hñt . v . car . Ibi moliñ de . ii . foliđ . Silua . i . leuu 7 dimiđ
long̃ . 7 dimiđ lat . T.R.E. ualb . viii . lib . Modo . iiii . lib.

Ipfe com teñ *ALVIDELEGE* . Algar tenuit . Ibi . i . hida.
Tra . ē . ix . car . In dñio funt . ii . 7 viii . uilli cū pbro 7 iiii.
borđ cū . vi . car . Ibi . vi . ač p̃ti . Silua . ii . leuu lg̃.

7 dimiđ lat.   T.R.E. ualb . vi . lib . Modo . c . foliđ.

Ipfe com teñ *COBINTONE* . 7 Rainalđ de eo.

Ibi . ii . hidæ . Tra . ē . iiii . car . In dñio funt . ii . 7 v . ferui.

7 iii . uilli 7 ii . libi hões cū . ii . car . 7 dimiđ . Ibi . xii . ač p̃ti.

T.R.E. ualb . xl . fol . 7 poft . ii . fol . Modo . xl . foliđ.

Hanc trā tenuit Almunđ 7 lib hō fuit.

Ipfe com tèn *HALAS* 7 Rainalđ de eo. IN *COLVESTAN* HĎ.
Algar tenuit . Ibi funt . ii . hidæ . Tra . ē . xv . car . In dñio
funt . iiii . car . 7 ii . ferui . 7 xxvi . uilli 7 xiiii . borđ 7 un niles
hñtes . x . car . Ibi moliñ de . iii . foliđ . 7 viii . ač p̃ti.

Silua . i . leuu 7 dimiđ lg̃ . 7 una leuu lat.

In hac uiila ht S Ebrulf . i . car cū pbro . q̃ ht . ii . boues.

Valet . viii . lib.

Hoc CO calūniat uicecom ad firmā regis . 7 comitatus
atteftatur qđ Eduuin tenuerit.

[In SEISDON Hundred]

1 Earl Roger holds CLAVERLEY. 20 hides. Earl Algar held it.
   Land for 32 ploughs. In lordship 5 ploughs;
      32 villagers and 13 smallholders who have 23 ploughs.
      A mill at 5s; meadow, 12 acres; woodland 2 leagues long
        and ½ league wide.
   Value before 1066 £7 10s; now £10.

  The Earl himself holds*
2 KINGSNORDLEY. Earl Algar held it. 2 hides. Land for 12 ploughs.
   In lordship 3 ploughs.
      7 villagers and 2 smallholders have 5 ploughs.
      A mill at 2s; woodland 1½ leagues long and ½ wide.
   Value before 1066 £8; now £4.

3 ALVELEY. Earl Algar held it. 1 hide. Land for 9 ploughs.
   In lordship 2;
      8 villagers with a priest and 4 smallholders with 6 ploughs.
      Meadow, 6 acres; woodland 2 leagues long and ½ wide.
   Value before 1066 £6; now 100s.

*4 'CUBBINGTON'. Reginald holds from him. 2 hides.
   Land for 4 ploughs. In lordship 2; 5 slaves;
      3 villagers and 2 free men with 2½ ploughs.
      Meadow, 12 acres.
   Value before 1066, 40s; later 2s; now 40s.
      Almund held this land. He was a free man.

  in CUTTLESTONE Hundred

5 (SHERIFF) HALES. Reginald holds from him. Earl Algar held it. 2 hides.
   Land for 15 ploughs. In lordship 4 ploughs; 2 slaves;
      26 villagers, 14 smallholders and 1 man-at-arms who have
        10 ploughs.
      A mill at 3s; meadow, 8 acres; woodland 1½ leagues long
        and 1 league wide.
   In this village St. Evroul's has 1 plough with a priest
      who has 2 oxen.*
   Value £8.
    The Sheriff claims this manor for the King's revenue; the
   County testifies that Earl Edwin held it. *

Ipſe cõm teñ *CHENISTELEI*.7 Rainald de eo. Bernulf

tenuit ut liƀ hõ. Ibi.ẽ una hida. Tra.ẽ. IIII. cař.

In dñio.ẽ dimiđ cař.7 VI. uiłłi 7 V. borđ hñt. II. cař.

Silua ibi. I. leuũ łg̃.7 dimiđ leuũ lat. Vał. X. ſoliđ.

Ipſe cõm teñ *MORTONE*.7 Benedict de eo.

Aluiet tenuit fine ſoca 7 ſaca. Ibi ſunt. II. hidæ. Tra.ẽ

III. cař. In dñio.ẽ una cař cũ. I. ſeruo.7 uñ miles cũ uno

anglico hñt. I. cař.7 IIII. borđ. Ibi moliñ de. XVI. denař.

Æccła S̃ EBRVLFI teñ *OTNE* de comite.

Ibi ſunt. II. hidæ. Tra.ẽ. V. cař. In dñio ſunt. III. cař.

7 uñ ſeruus.7 VII. uiłłi cũ. I. cař. Ibi. I. aĉ p̃ti. Silua

una leuũ łg̃.7 dimiđ lat. Hanc tr̃a Suain tenuit T.R.E.

Valet. IIII. liƀ.

Ipſa æccła teñ *MERTONE*. de comite. Vlgar tenuit 7 liƀ fuit.

Ibi.ẽ una hida. Tra.ẽ. X. cař. In dñio ſunt. IIII. cař.7 II.

ferui.7 IIII. uiłłi cũ. I. cař. Ibi. XII. aĉ p̃ti. In Stadford

XVIII. burg̃ſes p̃tiñ huic c̃ƆƆ. Quidã Walteri h̃t. I. cař ibi.

Valet. C. ſoliđ.

Ipſe cõm teñ *NORTBERIE* 7 Reger de eo. Alti tenuit ut

liƀ hõ. Ibi ſunt. II. hidæ 7 dim̃. Tra.ẽ. VIII. cař. In dñio

ſunt. II. cař. cũ. I. ſeruo.7 II. p̃bri 7 XIIII. uiłłi 7 IIII. borđ

cũ. VI. cař. Ibi. I. aĉ p̃ti. Silua. I. leuũ łg̃.7 dimiđ lat.

Valet. III. liƀ.

6 KNIGHTLEY. Reginald holds from him. Bernwulf held it as a
free man. 1 hide. Land for 4 ploughs. In lordship ½ plough.
   6 villagers and 5 smallholders have 2 ploughs.
   Woodland 1 league long and ½ league wide.
Value 10s.

7 MORETON (in Gnosall). Benedict holds from him. Alfgeat held it,
without full jurisdiction. 2 hides. Land for 3 ploughs.
In lordship 1 plough, with 1 slave.
   1 man-at-arms with 1 Englishman have 1 plough; 4 smallholders.
   A mill at 16d.
[Value...]

8 St. Evroul's Church holds (HIGH) ONN from the Earl. 2 hides.
Land for 5 ploughs. In lordship 3 ploughs; 1 slave;
   7 villagers with 1 plough.
   Meadow, 1 acre; woodland 1 league long and ½ wide.
   Swein, a free man, held this land before 1066.
Value £4.

[In PIREHILL Hundred]
9 This Church holds MARSTON (by Stafford) from the Earl.
Wulfgar held it; he was free. 1 hide. Land for 10 ploughs.
In lordship 4 ploughs; 2 slaves;
   4 villagers with 1 plough.
   Meadow, 12 acres.
   18 burgesses in Stafford belong to this manor.
       One Walter has 1 plough there.
Value 100s.

The Earl himself holds*
[in CUTTLESTONE Hundred]
10 NORBURY. Reger holds from him. Auti held it as a free man. 2½ hides.
Land for 8 ploughs. In lordship 2 ploughs with 1 slave;
   2 priests, 14 villagers and 4 smallholders with 6 ploughs.
   Meadow, 1 acre; woodland 1 league long and ½ wide.
Value £3.

Ipſe com̃ ten̄ *WALTONE* 7 Rogeri⁹ de eo. Almund tenuit.

Ibi ſunt . ıı . hidæ . Tra . e̅ . ııı . car̄ . In dn̄io ſunt . ıı . 7 ııı . ſerui.

7 v . uiłłi cũ . ı . car̄ . Ibi dimid̄ ac̃ p̃ti.   Valet . x . ſolid̄.

Ipſe com̃ ten̄ *ERLIDE* . 7 Rob̃t de eo. *IN PIREHOLLE HVND.*

Ibi . ı . hida cũ append̄ . Tra . e̅ . vı . car̄ . In dn̄io ſunt . ıı . car̄.

7 ıı . ſerui . 7 ıııı , uiłłi 7 ıııı . bord̄ cũ . ı . car̄ . Ibi . v . ac̃ p̃ti.

Valet . xxx . ſolid̄.

248 b

Ipſe com̃ ten̄ *GAITONE* . 7 Goisb̃t de eo . Ibi . ı . hida . Tra . e̅ . ıııı.

car̄ . In dn̄io . e̅ una . 7 x . uiłłi hn̄t . ıııı . car̄ . cũ . vı . bord̄.

Ibi . vɪ . ac̃ p̃ti . Silua . ı . leuũ łg̅ . 7 dimid̄ lat̄ . Val̄ . xxx . ſol̄.

Almar⁹ 7 Alric tenuer̄.

Ipſe com̃ ten̄ *COTE* . 7 Azelin⁹ de eo . Ibi . ıı . hidæ . Tra . e̅ . ıııı . car̄.

Ibi . e̅ . ı . car̄ 7 vı . boues cũ . ı . ſeruo . 7 ı . uiłło . Ibi . ıııı . ac̃ p̃ti.

Valet . xx . ſol̄ . Almund tenuit . 7 lib̄ fuit.

Ipſe com̃ ten̄ *COLTONE* . 7 Azelin⁹ de eo . Ibi . e̅ . ı . hida . Tra . e̅

ıııı . car̄ . Almund tenuit 7 lib̄ fuit . In dn̄io ſunt . ıı . car̄ . 7 ıııı.

ſerui . 7 xıııı . uiłłi cũ pb̃ro hn̄t . ııı . car̄ . Ibi . xvıı . ac̃ p̃ti.

Silua . ı . leuũ łg̅ . 7 dimid̄ lat̄ . Valet . xʟ . ſolid̄.

In *COLT* e̅ dimid̄ hida 7 p̃tin ad Coltone . Almar⁹ tenuit.

Ipſe com̃ ten̄ *RIDVARE* . 7 Azelin⁹ de eo . Ibi . ı . hida 7 dim̄.

Tra . e̅ . ıııı . car̄ . In dn̄io . e̅ una . 7 ıı . ſerui . cũ . ı . uiłło . Ibi . xvı.

ac̃ p̃ti . Silua . ı . leuũ łg̅ . 7 dim̄ . 7 tn̄td̄ lat̄ . Valet . xx . ſol̄.

Quinq̃ angli tenuer̄ . T.R.E . 7 adhuc hn̄t tra̅ . ıı . car̄ 7 dim̄.

1 WALTON (GRANGE). Roger holds from him. Almund held it. 2 hides.
Land for 3 ploughs. In lordship 2; 3 slaves;
   5 villagers with 1 plough.
   Meadow, ½ acre.
Value 10s.

in PIREHILL Hundred

2 YARLET. Robert holds from him. 1 hide, with its dependencies.
Land for 6 ploughs. In lordship 2 ploughs; 2 slaves;
   4 villagers and 4 smallholders with 1 plough.
   Meadow, 5 acres.
Value 30s.

3 GAYTON and AMERTON. Wulfric and Gosbert hold from him. 1 hide. 248 b
Land for 4 ploughs. In lordship 1.
   10 villagers have 4 ploughs with 6 smallholders.
   Meadow, 6 acres; woodland 1 league long and ½ wide.
Value 30s.
   Aelmer and Alric held them.

4 COTON (by Stafford). Ascelin holds from him. 2 hides.
Land for 4 ploughs. 1 plough and 6 oxen with 1 slave and
   1 villager.
   Meadow, 4 acres.
Value 20s.
   Almund held it; he was free.

5 COLTON. Ascelin holds from him. 1 hide. Land for 4 ploughs.
Almund held it; he was free. In lordship 2 ploughs; 4 slaves.
   14 villagers with a priest have 3 ploughs.
   Meadow, 19 acres; woodland 1 league long and ½ wide.
Value 40s.

6 In COLT there is ½ hide which belongs to Colton. Aelmer held it.

[in OFFLOW Hundred]

7 (MAVESYN) RIDWARE. Ascelin holds from him. 1½ hides.
Land for 4 ploughs. In lordship 1; 2 slaves with
   1 villager.
   Meadow, 16 acres; woodland 1½ leagues long and as wide.
Value 20s.
   5 Englishmen held it before 1066; they still have
land for 2½ ploughs.

Ipfe com̃ teñ *LOCHESLEI*.7 Azeliñ de eo.Ibi.iiii.pars
hidæ.Tra.ē.iiii.car.Vafta fuit 7 eft.Ibi.iiii.ac p̃ti.
Silua.i.leuū 7 dim̃ lg̃.7 dimid leuū lat̃.Val.x̱x.fol.
Edmund tenuit 7 lib̃ hō fuit.

Ipfe com̃ teñ *CRESSVALE* 7 Wills de eo.Ibi.ē.i.hida.
Tra.ē.vi.car.Ibi funt.iiii.uilli 7 iiii.bord cū.ii.car.
Ibi moliñ de.v.folid.7 xl.ac p̃ti.7 In Stadford una Vafta
mafura.   Valet.xx.fol.Goduiñ tenuit 7 lib̃ hō fuit.

Ipfe com̃ teñ *DODINTONE*.7 Wills de eo.Ibi.ē.i.hida.
Tra.ē.vi.car.Ibi funt.iii.uilli cū.i.car.Ibi.ii.ac p̃ti.
Silua.iiii.q̃rent lg̃.7 iii.q̃rent lat̃.Valet.xx.fol.
Suain tenuit.7 lib̃ hō fuit.

Ipfe com̃ teñ *MODREDESHALE*.7 Wills de eo.Ibi dim̃ hida.
Tra.ē.v.car.7 In codeuualle quæ ibi p̃tiñ.
Ibi funt.iii.uilli 7 ii.bord cū.i.car.7 iii.ac p̃ti.
Silua dim̃ leuū lg̃ 7 lat̃.   Val.x.folid.Godeua

Ipfe com̃ teñ *ALMENTONE*.7 Wills de eo.Ibi.iii.hidæ
cū append.Tra.ē.vi.car.In dñio.ē una.7 iiii.uilli 7 iiii.
bord cū.i.car.Ibi.ii.ac p̃ti.Silua.ii.leuū lg̃.7 una lat̃.
Valet.xxx.folid.Goduiñ tenuit 7 lib̃ hō fuit.

Ipfe com̃ teñ *TICHESHALE*.7 Henric de eo.Ibi dimid virg
træ.Tra.ē.iiii.car.In dñio.ē una car cū.i.uillo.Ibi.ii.ac
p̃ti.Silua.iii.q̃rent lg̃.7 ii.lat̃.Val.x.fol.Elmund.

[in TOTMONSLOW Hundred]

18 LOXLEY. Ascelin holds from him. The fourth part of 1 hide.
Land for 4 ploughs. It was and is waste.
    Meadow, 4 acres; woodland 1½ leagues long and ½ league wide.
Value 20s.
    Edmund held it; he was a free man.

[in PIREHILL Hundred]

19 CRESWELL. William Pandolf holds from him. 1 hide. Land for 6 ploughs.
    4 villagers and 4 smallholders with 2 ploughs.
    A mill at 5s; meadow, 40 acres.
    In Stafford, 1 unoccupied dwelling.
Value 20s.
    Godwin held it; he was a free man.

20 DERRINGTON. William holds from him. 1 hide. Land for 6 ploughs.
    3 villagers with 1 plough.
    Meadow, 2 acres; woodland 4 furlongs long and 3 furlongs wide.
Value 20s.
    Swein held it; he was a free man.

21 MODDERSHALL. William holds from him. ½ hide. Land for 5 ploughs;
in COTWALTON, which belongs there, land for...
    3 villagers and 2 smallholders with 1 plough.
    Meadow, 3 acres; woodland ½ league long and wide.
Value 10s.
    Godiva held it.

22 ALMINGTON. William holds from him. 3 hides with its dependencies.
Land for 6 ploughs. In lordship 1;
    4 villagers and 4 smallholders with 1 plough.
    Meadow, 2 acres; woodland 2 leagues long and 1 wide.
Value 30s.
    Godwin held it; he was a free man.

23 TIXALL. Henry of Ferrers holds from him. ½ virgate of land.
Land for 4 ploughs. In lordship 1 plough, with
    1 villager.
    Meadow, 2 acres; woodland 3 furlongs long and 2 wide.
Value 10s.
    Almund held it.

Ipſe coɱ teñ *METFORD*.7 Helgot de eo.Ibi.ē diɱ hida.

Tra.ē.ɪɪɪɪ.car.In dñio.ē una.cū.ɪ.ſeruo.7 v.uiłłi 7 ɪɪ.

bord cū.ɪ.car.Ibi.ɪɪ.ac p̃ti.Vał.xxx.ſolid.Suain tenuit. *lib ſuit*

Ipſe coɱ teñ *ESSELIE*.7 Goisfrid de eo.Ibi.ɪɪ.hidæ

Tra.ē.ɪɪɪ.car.In dñio.ē una.7 ɪɪ.uiłłi 7 ɪɪ.bord

Silua ibi.ɪ.leuu lḡ.7 diɱ lat.Vał.xv.ſoł.Vlmar tenuit. *lib ſuit.*

Ipſe coɱ teñ *RIDVARE*.7 Walter de eo.Ibi.ɪ.virḡ træ.

Tra.ē.ɪ.car 7 dimid.Ibi ſunt.ɪɪ.ſerui 7 ɪɪɪɪ.uiłłi.7 ɪɪɪɪ.

ac p̃ti.Silua.ɪ.leuu lḡ.7 dimid lat.Valet.v.ſolid.

Edmund tenuit.7 lib hō fuit.

Ipſe coɱ teñ *BLIDEVELT*.7 Roger de eo.Ibi.ē.ɪ.hida.Tra.ē

.ɪɪɪɪ.car.In dñio ſt.ɪɪ.car.7 ɪɪɪɪ.ſerui.7 vɪɪ.uiłłi cū p̃bro 7 ɪ.bord.

hñt.ɪɪ.car.Ibi.vɪ.ac p̃ti.Silua ht.ɪɪɪ.q̃ɀ lḡ.7 una q̃ɀ lat.

Valet.xx.ſolid.Edmund tenuit.7 lib hō fuit.

Ipſe coɱ teñ *ÆNESTANEFELT*.7 Wiłłs de eo.Ibi ſunt.ɪɪɪ.

virḡ træ.Tra.ē.ɪɪɪ.car.In dñio.ē una.7 uñ uiłłs cū.ɪ.car.

In Wereſlei quæ p̃tiñ huic ꟲ ē tra   Ibi ſunt   ſ

ɪɪɪɪ.uiłłi 7 ɪɪ.bord cū.ɪ.car.Ibi.vɪɪɪ.ac p̃ti.Silua ibi

una leuu lḡ.7 dimid lat.Vał.xL.ſoł.Goduiñ tenuit.

4 MEAFORD. Helgot holds from him. ½ hide. Land for 4 ploughs.
In lordship 1, with 1 slave;
    5 villagers and 2 smallholders with 1 plough.
    Meadow, 2 acres.
Value 30s.
    Swein held it; he was free.

5 ASHLEY. Geoffrey holds from him. 2 hides. Land for 3 ploughs.
In lordship 1;
    2 villagers and 2 smallholders.
    Woodland 1 league long and ½ wide.
Value 15s.
    Wulfmer held it; he was free.

[in OFFLOW Hundred]
6 (HAMSTALL) RIDWARE. Walter holds from him. 1 virgate of land.
Land for 1½ ploughs. 2 slaves;
    4 villagers.
    Meadow, 4 acres; woodland 1 league long and ½ wide.
Value 5s.
    Edmund held it; he was a free man.

[in PIREHILL Hundred]
7 BLITHFIELD. Roger holds from him. 1 hide. Land for 4 ploughs.
In lordship 2 ploughs, 4 slaves.
    7 villagers with a priest and 1 smallholder have 2 ploughs.
    Meadow, 6 acres; the woodland has 3 furlongs length and
        1 furlong width.
Value 20s.
    Edmund held it; he was a free man.

[in TOTMONSLOW Hundred]
8 ALSTONFIELD. William holds from him. 3 virgates of land.
Land for 3 ploughs. In lordship 1;
    1 villager with 1 plough.
[Value...]

9 In WARSLOW, which belongs to this manor, land for......*   r
    4 villagers and 2 smallholders with 1 plough.
    Meadow, 8 acres; woodland 1 league long and ½ wide.
Value 40s.
    Godwin held it.

Ipſe com̄ teñ *CELTETONE*.7 Wiłłs de eo.Ibi.ē dimiđ hida.
Tra.ē.IIII.caŕ.In dñio.ē dimiđ caŕ.7 III.uiłłi 7 I.borđ cū dim̄
╱caŕ.

248 c

Silua dimiđ leūu lḡ.7 III.q̄renť lať.

In *BECHESWORD* quæ.ptiñ ad ipsū m̄ eſt dimiđ hida.Ibi ſunt
IIII.uiłłi 7 I.borđ.cū.I.caŕ.Ibi.I.ač p̃ti.Silua.II.leūu lḡ.
7 una leūu 7 dim̄ lať.Toť uał.xv.foliđ.Goduiñ tenuit.7 lib̄ fuit.
Iſđ Comes teñ *SENESTE*.7 Rob̄t de eo. IN*OFFELAV HVND*.
Ibi ſunt.III.hiđ.Tra.ē.XII.caŕ.In dñio ſunt.II.caŕ.cū.I.ſeruo.
7 XXI.uiłłs 7 IIII.borđ cū XIIII.caŕ.Ibi moliñ de.LXVI.deñ.
7 una ač p̃ti.Silua.III.leūu lḡ.7 una 7 dim̄ leūu lať.Valet
.c.foliđ.Goduiñ tenuit.7 lib̄ hō fuit.

.VIII. **H**TERRA HVGONIS DE MONTGVMERI.
Hvgo de Montgumeri teñ de rege *WRFELD*.Algar tenuit.
Ibi.xxx.hidæ.Terra.ē.xxx.caŕ.In dñio ſunt.IIII.7 v.ſerui.
7 LXVII.uiłłi cū pb̄ro 7 x.borđ hñt.xxv.caŕ.Ibi.III.molini
de.xL.foliđ.7 piſcaria de.xv.foliđ.7 xvi.ač p̃ti.Silua.III.leūu
lḡ.7 una lať.Ibi.III.angli hñt.v.caŕ.cū.xviii.uiłłis.7 v.borđ.
Valuit.III.lib̄.Modo.xviii.lib̄.De hac ťra ſuꝗ.III.hidæ Vaſtæ.

.IX. **H**TERRA HENRICI DE FERIERES. IN*PIREHOLLE HVND*.
Henricvs de Ferreres h̄ŧ caſtellū de *TOTEBERIE*.
In Burgo circa caſtellū ſunt.xLII.hōes de mercato ſuo tanť
uiuentes.7 reddt çū foro.IIII.lib̄.7 x.foliđ.
In *BVRTONE* h̄ŧ dimiđ hidā.in qua ſeđ eꝗ caſtellū.In qua
T.R.E.erant.xII.caŕ.Ibi ſunt m̄.IIII.caŕ in dñio.
Val p anñ.xx.IIII.foliđ.   IN*OFFELAV HVND*.
Ipſe Henriç teñ *ROLVESTVNE*.Morcar tenuit.Ibi.II.hidæ
7 dimiđ.Tra.ē.vIII.caŕ.In dñio ſunt.IIII.caŕ.7 I.ancilla.

The Earl holds CHEDDLETON himself, and William from him. ½ hide.
Land for 4 ploughs. In lordship ½ plough;
   3 villagers and 1 smallholder with ½ plough.
   Woodland ½ league long and 3 furlongs wide.   248 c

In BASFORD, which belongs to this manor, is ½ hide.
   4 villagers and 1 smallholder with 1 plough.
   Meadow, 1 acre. Woodland 2 leagues long and 1½ leagues wide.
Total value 15s.
   Godwin held it; he was free.

In OFFLOW Hundred
Earl Roger also holds SHENSTONE and Robert d'Oilly from him. 3 hides.
Land for 12 ploughs. In lordship 2 ploughs with 1 slave;
   21 villagers and 4 smallholders with 14 ploughs.
   A mill at 66d; meadow, 1 acre; woodland 3 leagues long
      and 1½ leagues wide.
Value 100s.
   Godwin held it; he was a free man.

LAND OF HUGH OF MONTGOMERY

[In SEISDON Hundred]

Hugh of Montgomery holds WORFIELD from the King. Earl Algar
held it. 30 hides. Land for 30 ploughs. In lordship 4; 5 slaves.
   67 villagers with a priest and 10 smallholders have 25 ploughs.
   3 mills at 40s; a fishery at 15s; meadow, 16 acres;
      woodland 3 leagues long and 1 wide.
   3 Englishmen have 5 ploughs with 18 villagers and 5 smallholders.
The value was £3; now £18.
   3 hides of this land are waste.

LAND OF HENRY OF FERRERS

In [OFFLOW] Hundred*
Henry of Ferrers has TUTBURY Castle. In the Borough around
the castle are 42 men who live only by their trading; with
the market, they pay £4 10s.

In BURTON he has ½ hide in which his castle stands, where
there were 12 ploughs before 1066; now 4 ploughs in lordship.
Value 24s a year.

In OFFLOW Hundred
Henry holds ROLLESTON himself. Earl Morcar held it. 2½ hides.
Land for 8 ploughs. In lordship 4 ploughs; 1 female slave;

7 xviii.uilli 7 xvi.bord cū pͫbro hñtes.xiiii.car.Ibi moliñ
de.v.folid.Ibi.ʟ.aͨ p̃ti.Silua paſtil.iii.leuu l͡g.7 ii.leuu
lat.Tra arabil.ii.leuu l͡g.7 una lat.Valet.x.lib.

Ipſe.H.ten MERCHAMETONE.Ibi.ii.hidæ.7 In Edgareſlege
una v̄ træ.Vluric tenuit.7 lib hō fuit.Tra.ē vii.car.

In dñio funt.ii.cū.i.feruo.7 xviii.uilli 7 ix.bord cū.iii.car.
Ibi.xʟ.aͨ p̃ti.Silua paſtil.iii.leuu l͡g.7 una leuu 7 dim
lat.Valet.c.folid.

Ipſe.H.ten DRAICOTE.Ibi dimid hida.Tra.ē.i.car
In dñio.ē ipſa car.7 iiii.uilli 7 iiii.bord hñt.i.car.
Ibi.xii.aͨ p̃ti.Silua dimid leuu l͡g.7 tntd lat.Val.xv.fol.

Ipſe.H.ten FELEDE.7 Hubt de eo.Ibi dimid hida
Tra.ē.i.car.In dñio.ē ipſa.7 ibi funt.vi.bord.Valet.xv.fol.
In ead uilla ten Rogeri de.H.dimid hidā.Tra.ē dimid car.
Ibi pͫbr hͫ.i.car.7 ibi.ii.bord.Ibi.ē.i.hida.quā iſti.ii.ten.
Ibi.ʟ.aͨ p̃ti.Silua paſtil.iii.leuu l͡g.7 i.leuu lat.
Valet.xv.folid.

Totā h̄ uillā FELEDE.tenuit T.R.E.Sͨa Wareburg de ceſtre.
Ipſe.H.ten MORTVNE.7 Alcher de eo.Ibi.i.virg træ.
Tra.ē dim car.Ibi funt.iii.uilli cū.i.car.Ibi.xii.aͨ p̃ti.
Silua.i.leuu in l͡g 7 lat.Tres libi hoes tenuer.

18 villagers and 16 smallholders with a priest who have 14 ploughs.
A mill at 5s; meadow, 50 acres; woodland pasture 3 leagues
   long and 2 leagues wide; arable land 2 leagues long and 1 wide.
Value £10.

4 Henry holds MARCHINGTON himself. 2 hides. 1 virgate of land
in AGARDSLEY. Wulfric held it; he was a free man.
Land for 7 ploughs. In lordship 2, with 1 slave;
   18 villagers and 9 smallholders with 3 ploughs.
Meadow, 40 acres; woodland pasture 3 leagues long and
   1½ leagues wide.
Value 100s.

5 Henry holds DRAYCOTT himself. ½ hide. Land for 1 plough.
In lordship, this plough.
   4 villagers and 4 smallholders have 1 plough.
Meadow, 12 acres; woodland ½ league long and as wide.
Value 15s.

6 Henry holds FAULD himself, and Hubert from him. ½ hide.
Land for 1 plough. It is in lordship.
   6 smallholders.
Value 15s.

*7 In the same village Roger holds ½ hide from Henry. Land for ½ plough.
   A priest has 1 plough; 2 smallholders. 1 hide there, which
      these two hold.
Meadow, 50 acres; woodland pasture 3 leagues long
   and 1 league wide.
Value 15s.
   Before 1066 St. Werburgh's of Chester held the whole of this
village of Fauld.

8 Henry holds MORETON (in Hanbury) himself, and Alchere from him. 1
virgate of land. Land for ½ plough.
   3 villagers with 1 plough.
Meadow, 12 acres; woodland 1 league in length and width.
[Value...]
   Three free men held it.

Ipſe.H.teñ *CEBBESIO*.7 Hunfrid de eo.Ibi.v.hidæ.
Tra.ē.xii.car.In dñio ſunt.iii.7 viii.ſerui.7 xx.uitti
cū pƀro 7 ix.borđ hñt.viii.car.Ibi.xx.ac̄ p̃ti.Silua
paſtit.ii.q̃rent l̄g.7 una lat. Valet.iiii.liƀ.
Ad hoc ꝏ ꝑtinuit tra de Stadford.in qua rex p̃cepit
fieri caſtellū qđ m̄ eſt deſtruc̄tū.
In uilla de Burtone h̄t Radulf miles henrici.i.car in
dñio.7 iii.borđ cū.i.car.Ibi ſunt.xx.ac̄ p̃ti.
Silua.iiii.q̃rent l̄g.7 tñtđ lat.

248 d

.XI. **TERRA ROBERTI DE STATFORD** *IN PEREOLLE HVND*

R OTBERTVS De STADFORD teñ *TILLINTONE*.Tol tenuit.
7 liƀ hō fuit.Ibi.iii.hidæ.Tra.iiii.car.Ibi ſunt.v.uitti 7 ii.
borđ cū.ii.car.Ibi.iiii.ac̄ p̃ti.Valet.xxx.ſoliđ. *IN TAMENASLAV*
Ipſe Roƀt teñ *TENE*.Vluiet 7 Vlmer tenuer̄.7 liƀi fuer̄. . *HVND*.
Ibi dimiđ hida.Tra.ē.vi.car.Ibi ſunt.vi.uitt 7 vi.borđ cū iii.
car.7 iii.ſerui.Ibi.vi.ac̄ p̃ti.Silua.i.leuu l̄g.7 dimiđ lat.
Valet.xxx.ſoliđ.
Ipſe.R.teñ in *GRENDONE*.tciā parte uni hidæ.Vaſta.ē.
Vluiet tenuit.T.R.E.
Ipſe.R.teñ in *CALDONE*.unā virg.træ.Tra.ē.i.car.Vaſta.ē.
Godeua tenuit T.R.E.
Ipſe.R.teñ in *BVGHALE*.unā v træ.quæ ꝑtiñ ad *HALSTONE*.
Tra.ē.i.car.Vlmar tenuit 7 liƀ hō fuit.Ibi ſunt.ii.uitti cū.i.
car.7 ii.ac̄ ſiluæ.Vat.v.ſot.

248 c, d

[In PIREHILL Hundred]

9 Henry holds CHEBSEY himself and Humphrey from him. 5 hides.
Land for 12 ploughs. In lordship 3; 8 slaves.
    20 villagers with a priest and 9 smallholders have 8 ploughs.
    Meadow, 20 acres; woodland pasture 2 furlongs long and
        1 wide.
Value £4.
    To this manor belonged Stafford land on which the King ordered
a castle to be made; it has now been destroyed.

[? In OFFLOW Hundred ?]

10 In the village of BURTON Ralph, one of Henry's men-at-arms,
has 1 plough in lordship;
    3 smallholders with 1 plough.
    Meadow, 20 acres; woodland 4 furlongs long and as wide.
    [Value...]

1   LAND OF ROBERT OF STAFFORD*   248 d

In PIREHILL Hundred

1 Robert of Stafford holds TILLINGTON. Tholf held it; he was
a free man. 3 hides. Land for 4 ploughs.
    5 villagers and 2 smallholders with 2 ploughs.
    Meadow, 4 acres.
Value 30s.

Robert himself holds*

in TOTMONSLOW Hundred

2 TEAN. Wulfgeat and Wulfmer held it; they were free. ½ hide.
Land for 6 ploughs.
    6 villagers and 6 smallholders with 3 ploughs and 3 slaves.
    Meadow, 6 acres; woodland 1 league long and ½ wide.
Value 30s.

3 in GRINDON the third part of 1 hide. Waste. Wulfgeat
held it before 1066.

4 in CAULDON 1 virgate of land. Land for 1 plough. Waste.
Godiva held it before 1066.

[in CUTTLESTONE Hundred]

5 in BROUGH HALL, 1 virgate of land, which belongs to Haughton.
Land for 1 plough. Wulfmer held it; he was a free man.
    2 villagers with 1 plough.
    Woodland 2 acres.
Value 5s.

Ipſe.R.teñ BRADELIA cū appendic.Edduin tenuit.Tra.ē

xliiii.car.int oms berew.In Bradelie.i.hida tñt.

Ibi.ē in dñio.i.car.⁊ ii.ſerui.⁊ xii.uilti.⁊ iiii.borđ.cū.xi.car.

Ibi moliñ de.v.ſoł.⁊ xii.ac p̃ti.Silua.i.leuu lḡ.⁊ dimiđ lať.

In Bernertone.i.hida.In Abetone.ii.hidæ.In Lvtiudæ.i.hida.

In Belintone.ii.hidæ.In Burtone.ii.hidæ ⁊ dim.In Selchemore.i.hiđ

In Longenalre.i.hiđ.In Mutone.ii.hidæ.In Aluerdeſtone.i.hiđ.

In Vllaueſtone.ii.hidæ.   Hæ træ p̃tiñ ad Bradelie.

In his ſunt.xlviii.uilti.⁊ xxvi.borđ.hñtes.xvii.car.

⁊ In dñio.ē una.In Aluerdeſtone.⁊ q̇đā miles.⁊ xv.ac p̃ti.

Totū ꝳ cū mēbris uał.vii.liƀ.   ſregis.

In Burgo de STATFORD hŧ Roƀt.lxx.ſoł.de medietate partis

Ipſe.R.teñ WALETONE.⁊ Ernalđ de eo. IN PIREHOLLE HĐ.

Ibi.iii.hidæ.Tra.ē.vi.caŕ.In dñio.ē una.⁊ vii.uilti ⁊ ii.borđ ⁊ v.

ſerui cū pƀro hñtes.iiii.caŕ.Silua.ii.q̇rent lḡ.⁊ una lať.⁊ p̃tū

ſimiliť.Vał.lx.ſoliđ.Achil tenuit ⁊ unā car træ huj ſorori ſuæ deđ.

Ipſe.R.teñ in ESTONE.tres partes uni hidæ.Sex taini tenueŕ

⁊ liƀi fueŕ.Tra.ē.viii.caŕ.In dñio ſunt.ii.caŕ.⁊ vii.uilti ⁊ iiii.

borđ cū.i.ſeruo hñtes.v.caŕ.Silua.ii.q̇renť lḡ.⁊ una q̇ʒ lať.

⁊ tñtđ p̃ti.Vał.lxx.ſoł.Cadio teñ de Roƀto.

*6 BRADLEY, with its dependencies. Earl Edwin held it. Land
for 44 ploughs, between all the outliers; in Bradley 1 hide only.
In lordship 1 plough; 2 slaves;
12 villagers and 4 smallholders with 11 ploughs.
A mill at 5s; meadow, 12 acres; woodland 1 league long
and ½ wide.
In BARTON 1 hide; in APETON 2 hides; in LITTYWOOD 1 hide;
in BILLINGTON 2 hides; in BURTON 2½ hides; in SILKMORE
1 hide; in LONGNOR 1 hide; in MITTON 2 hides;
in ALSTONE 1 hide; in WOOLLASTON 2 hides.
These lands belong to Bradley. In them are
48 villagers and 26 smallholders who have 17 ploughs.
In lordship 1, in Alstone, and a man-at-arms; meadow 15 acres.
Value of whole manor, with its members, £7.

7 In the Borough of STAFFORD Robert has 70s from his half of
the King's part.*

Robert himself holds*
In PIREHILL Hundred
8 WALTON (in Stone). Arnold holds from him. 3 hides. Land
for 6 ploughs. In lordship 1;
7 villagers, 2 smallholders and 5 slaves with a priest
who have 4 ploughs.
Woodland 2 furlongs long and 1 wide; meadow, the same.
Value 60s.
Aki, a free man, held it; he gave 1 carucate of this land
to his sister.

9 in ASTON and STOKE (by-Stone), three parts of 1 hide. 6 thanes
held it; they were free. Land for 8 ploughs. In lordship 2 ploughs;
7 villagers and 4 smallholders with 1 slave who have 5 ploughs.
Woodland 2 furlongs long and 1 furlong wide; as much meadow.
Value 70s.
Cadio holds from Robert.

Ipſe.R.teñ in parua SANDONE.I.virg̃ træ.7|Cadio de eo.

Hanc tenueꝛ Aluuiñ 7 Aluuiñ 7 Wicſtric.Duo eoꝣ libi fueꝛ.

Wiſtric cū tra diſcedere ñ poterat.In hac virg̃.ē tra.IIII.caꝛ.

In dñio.ē una.7 IIII.uiłłi 7 II.borđ.cū.II.caꝛ.Ibi.XIIII.ac̃ p̃ti.

Valet.X.ſoliđ.

Ipſe.R.teñ in HOTONE.II.hiđ.Aluuarđ tenuit.7 lib hō fuit.

Tra.ē.VI.caꝛ.In dñio ſunt.II.caꝛ.7 VI.uiłłi 7 IIII.borđ 7 II.ſerui.

cū.III.caꝛ 7 dimiđ.Ibi.IIII.ac̃ p̃ti.Silua modica.II.q̃rent lg̃.

7 dimiđ lat̃.Valet.XL.ſoliđ.Gißłebt teñ de Robto.

Ipſe.R.teñ in SELTE.II.hiđ.7 Gißłebt de eo.Has tenueꝛ Leuuiñ

eꝓs 7 Ormaꝛ.ſed ſacā 7 ſocā huj.O.habuit rex.Tra.ē.IIII.caꝛ.

Ibi.ē una caꝛ.7 VI.uiłłi 7 IIII.borđ.7 II.   Ibi moliñ de.III.

ſoł.7 XII.ac̃ p̃ti.7 IIII.ac̃ ſiluæ.Vał.X.ſoliđ.

Ipſe.R.teñ in CISEWORDE 7 in Ceppecanole.II.hiđ.7 Gißłebt

teñ de eo.Tra.ē.VI.caꝛ.In dñio ſunt.II.caꝛ.7 XII.uiłłi 7 VIII.

borđ cū.III.caꝛ.7 dimiđ.Ibi.I.ac̃ p̃ti.Silua.II.leúu lg̃.7 dimiđ

lat̃.Valet.XL.ſoliđ.Godeua tenuit.ſed de ceppecanole

reddeb.II.ſoliđ.æcclæ S̃ Cedde.

Ipſe.R.teñ.I.hiđ in OFFELIE.7 Vrfer de eo.Vluric̃ tenuit.7 lib

fuit.Tra.ē.IIII.caꝛ.In dñio ſunt.II.cū.I.ſeruo.7 IIII.uiłłi 7 IIII.

borđ.cū.II.caꝛ.Ibi.VIII.ac̃ p̃ti.Silua hꝉ.I.leúu lg̃.7 dim lat̃.

Valet.XL.ſoliđ.

Ipſe.R.teñ.II.hiđ in STANTONE.7 in RIGGE.7 Briend de eo.

Siuuarđ tenuit.7 lib hō fuit.Tra.ē.VI.caꝛ.In dñio.ē una.

7 XI.uiłłi 7 III.borđ 7 III.ſerui cū.V.caꝛ.Ibi pbr 7 moliñ de.V.ſoł.

Ibi.II.ac̃ p̃ti.7 XIIII.ac̃ grauæ.Valet.XL.ſoliđ.

10   in 'LITTLE SANDON' 1 virgate of land. Cadio also holds from him.
Alwin, Alwin and Wihtric held it; two of them were free.
Wihtric could not leave with the land. In this virgate, land
for 4 ploughs. In lordship 1;
    4 villagers and 2 smallholders with 2 ploughs.
    Meadow, 14 acres.
Value 10s.

11   in HOPTON 2 hides. Alfward held it; he was a free man.
Land for 6 ploughs. In lordship 2 ploughs;
    6 villagers, 4 smallholders and 2 slaves with 3½ ploughs.
    Meadow, 4 acres; a small wood 2 furlongs long and ½ wide.
Value 40s.
    Gilbert holds from Robert.

12   in SALT 2 hides. Gilbert holds from him. Bishop Leofwin* and
Ordmer held them* but the King had the full jurisdiction of
this Ordmer. Land for 4 ploughs. 1 plough there;
    6 villagers, 4 smallholders and 2.....*
A mill at 3s; meadow, 12 acres; woodland, 4 acres.
Value 10s.

13   in CHESWARDINE and in CHIPNALL 2 hides; Gilbert holds from him.
Land for 6 ploughs. In lordship 2 ploughs;
    12 villagers and 8 smallholders with 3½ ploughs.
    Meadow, 1 acre. Woodland 2 leagues long and ½ wide.
Value 40s.
    Godiva held it, but she paid 2s from Chipnall to St. Chad's Church.

14   in [HIGH] OFFLEY 1 hide. Urfer holds from him. Wulfric held it;
he was free. Land for 4 ploughs. In lordship 2, with 1 slave;
    4 villagers and 4 smallholders with 2 ploughs.
    Meadow, 8 acres; woodland 1 league long and ½ wide.*
Value 40s.

15   in STANDON and in THE RUDGE 2 hides. Bryant holds from him.
Siward held it; he was a free man. Land for 6 ploughs. In lordship 1;
    11 villagers, 3 smallholders and 3 slaves with 5 ploughs. A priest.
    A mill at 5s; meadow, 2 acres; copse, 14 acres.
Value 40s.

Ipſe.R.ten̄ in *WESTONE* unā v̄ træ.⁊ Briend de eo.Goduin̄
tenuit ⁊ lib̄ fuit.Tra.ē.ıı.car̄.In dn̄io.ē una car̄.⁊ vı.ſerui.
⁊ ıııı.uilli ⁊ ıı.bord̄ cū.ı.car̄.Silua.dimid̄ leuu lḡ.⁊ ıı.q̄ᵹ lat̄.

⟨Valet.xx.ſol.

Ipſe ten̄ unā v̄ træ in *MERE*.⁊ Vluiet de eo.Ipſe tenuit.
⁊ lib̄ hō fuit.Tra.ē.ıı.car̄.Ibi ſunt.ıııı.uilli ⁊ ı.bord̄ cū.ı.car̄.
Silua.ı.leuu lḡ.⁊ altera lat̄.Val̄.x.ſolid̄.
Iſd̄.R.ten̄.ıı.hid̄ in *SVLVERTONE*.⁊ Aſlen de eo.Broder
tenuit ⁊ lib̄ hō fuit.Tra.ē.vııı.car̄.In dn̄io.ē una.⁊ x.uilli
⁊ v.bord̄ cū.vı.car̄.Ibi.x.ac̄ p̄ti.Silua.ı.leuu lḡ.⁊ ı.lat̄.
Valet.xl.ſolid̄.
Ipſe.R.ten̄.ıı.hid̄ in *NORTONE* ⁊ in appendic̄.Godric̄
⁊ Vluiet tenuer̄.libi q̄ fuer̄.Tra.ē.ıııı.car̄.Ibi ſunt.vı.uilli
⁊ ııı.bord̄.cū.ııı.car̄.Silua.ııı.leuu lḡ.⁊ ıı.leuu lat̄.
Valet.xl.ſolid̄.
Ipſe.R.ten̄ in *MADELIE*.ı.hidā.⁊ Vluiet de eo.Suain
tenuit ⁊ lib̄ hō fuit.Tra.ē.ıııı.car̄.In dn̄io.ē una car̄.
⁊ v.uilli ⁊ vıı.bord̄ cū.ıı.car̄.Silua.ı.leuu ⁊ dim̄ lḡ.⁊ ı.leuu
lat̄.Val̄.xxx.ſolid̄.
Iſd̄.R.ten̄ in *HELTONE* ⁊ in *RISCTONE*.tciā parte.ı.hidæ.
⁊ Vluiet ten̄ de eo.Ipſe tenuit.T.R.E.Tra.ē.ııı.car̄.Ibi ſunt
ııı.uilli ⁊ ııı.bord̄.cū.ı.car̄.Silua.ı.leuu lḡ.⁊ dim̄ lat̄.
Valet.x.ſolid̄.

6 in WESTON (in Standon) 1 virgate of land. Bryant holds from him.
Godwin held it; he was free. Land for 2 ploughs. In lordship 1
plough; 6 slaves;
    4 villagers and 2 smallholders with 1 plough.
    Woodland ½ league long and 2 furlongs wide.
Value 20s.

7 in MAER 1 virgate of land. Wulfgeat holds from him. He held   249 a
it himself; he was a free man. Land for 2 ploughs.
    4 villagers and 1 smallholder with 1 plough.
    Woodland 1 league long and another wide.
Value 10s.

8 Robert also holds 2 hides in SWYNNERTON. Aslen holds from him.
Broder held it; he was a free man. Land for 8 ploughs.
In lordship 1;
    10 villagers and 5 smallholders with 6 ploughs.
    Meadow, 10 acres; woodland 1 league long and 1 wide.
Value 40s.

9 Robert holds 2 hides himself in NORTON (-in-the-Moors) and in
its dependencies. Godric and Wulfgeat, who were free, held it.
Land for 4 ploughs.
    6 villagers and 3 smallholders with 3 ploughs.
    Woodland 3 leagues long and 2 leagues wide.
Value 40s.

20 Robert holds 1 hide himself in (GREAT) MADELEY. Wulfgeat holds
from him. Swein held it; he was a free man. Land for 4 ploughs.
In lordship 1 plough;
    5 villagers and 7 smallholders with 2 ploughs.
    Woodland 1½ leagues long and 1 league wide.
Value 30s.

21 Robert also holds the third part of 1 hide in (ABBEY) HULTON
and RUSHTON (GRANGE). Wulfgeat holds from him. He
held it himself before 1066. Land for 3 ploughs.
    3 villagers and 3 smallholders with 1 plough.
    Woodland 1 league long and ½ wide.
Value 10s.

Ipſe.R.ten in *BARCARDESLIM* tciā partē.ɪ.hidæ.Al
uuard tenuit.7 lib̄ hō fuit.Tra.ē.ɪɪ.car̄.Ibi.ē un̄ uilłs
7 ɪɪɪɪ.borđ cū.ɪ.car̄.Ibi.ɪɪ.ac̄ alneti.Val.x.ſoliđ.
Vluiet tenuit.
Ipſo.R.ten.ɪ.hiđ in *ESTONE* 7 appendic̄.7 Ælgot de eo.
Godeua 7 Edric̄ tenuer̄ 7 libi fuer̄.Tra.ē.ɪɪɪ.car̄.Ibi
ſunt.ɪɪɪ.borđ cū.ɪ.car̄.Silua.ɪ.leuu lḡ.7 dimiđ leuu lat̄.
Valet.x.ſoliđ.
Iſđ.R.ten in *BERNVLVESTONE* dimiđ hidā.7 Helgot de eo.
Auguſtin tenuit 7 lib̄ hō fuit.Tra.ē.vɪ.car̄.In dñio.ē una.
cū.ɪ.ſeruo.7 ɪɪɪɪ.uilłi 7 ɪɪɪ.borđ cū.ɪ.car̄.Ibi.vɪ.ac̄ p̄ti.7 ɪɪɪ.ac̄
ſiluæ.Valet.xL.ſoliđ.
Iſđ.R.ten in *RANTONE* dimiđ hiđ.7 Godric̄ de eo.qui 7 tenuit
ut lib̄ hō.Tra.ē.ɪɪ.car̄.In dñio.ē una.7 vɪ.uilłi 7 v.borđ hn̄t
ɪɪɪ.car̄.Ibi.ɪɪɪ.ac̄ p̄ti.Silua.ɪ.leuu lḡ.7 dimiđ lat̄.Val.xx.ſol.
Ipſe.R.ten in *CVCHESLAND* dim̄ hiđ 7 Helio de eo.Tochi 7 Aluric
tenuer̄ 7 libi fuer̄.Tra.ē.ɪɪ.car̄.Ibi.ɪ.uilłs 7.ɪɪ.borđ.7 v.ac̄ p̄ti.
Silua.ɪɪ.q̄rent lḡ.7 una lat̄.Valet.vɪ.ſoliđ.
Ipſe.R.ten in *HELDVLVES TONE* q̄ntā partē uni hidæ
Dūning 7 Vluric tenuer̄ 7 libi hoēs fuer̄.Tra.ē.ɪɪɪ.car̄.In
dñio.ē una.7 ɪɪ.uilłi 7 ɪɪ.borđ 7 ɪɪ.ſerui.cū.ɪ.car̄.7 una
ac̄ p̄ti.Silua.ɪ.leuu lḡ.7 dimiđ lat̄.Valet.x.ſoliđ.
Vitalis ten de Robto.

22 Robert holds the third part of 1 hide himself in BURSLEM.
Alfward held it; he was a free man. Land for 2 ploughs.
   1 villager and 4 smallholders with 1 plough.
   Alder grove, 2 acres.
Value 10s.
   Wulfgeat held it.

23 Robert holds 1 hide himself in ASTON (-by-Stone), and its
dependencies, and Algot from him. Godiva and Edric held it;
they were free. Land for 3 ploughs.
   3 smallholders with 1 plough.
   Woodland 1 league long and ½ league wide.
Value 10s.

24 Robert also holds ½ hide in BARLASTON, and Helgot from him.
Augustine held it; he was a free man. Land for 6 ploughs.
In lordship 1, with 1 slave;
   4 villagers and 3 smallholders with 1 plough.
   Meadow, 6 acres; woodland, 3 acres.
Value 40s.

25 Robert also holds ½ hide in RANTON. Godric, who held it as
a free man, holds from him. Land for 2 ploughs. In lordship 1.
   6 villagers and 5 smallholders have 3 ploughs.
   Meadow, 3 acres; woodland 1 league long and ½ wide.
Value 20s.

26 Robert holds ½ hide himself in COOKSLAND, and Helio from him.
Toki and Aelfric held it; they were free. Land for 2 ploughs.
   1 villager and 2 smallholders.
   Meadow, 5 acres; woodland 2 furlongs long and 1 wide.
Value 6s.

27 Robert holds the fifth part of 1 hide himself in HILDERSTONE.
Dunning and Wulfric held it; they were free men. Land for 3 ploughs.
In lordship 1;
   2 villagers, 2 smallholders and 2 slaves with 1 plough.
   Meadow, 1 acre; woodland 1 league long and ½ wide.
Value 10s.
   Vitalis holds from Robert.

Iſd . R . ten in *BRADELIE* diɱ hiđ 7 Tanio de eo . Vluuiet
7 Aluuard tenueꝛ . 7 libi fueꝛ . Tra . ē . iiii . caꝛ . In dñio . ē una.
7 iii . ſerui . 7 iii . uiłłi 7 vi . borđ . cū . ii . caꝛ . Ibi . iiii . ac̄ p̄ti.
Silua . ii . leúu lḡ . 7 una laꝵ . Valet . xl . ſoł.
Iſd . R . ten in *COLTVNE* . i . hiđ 7 Goisfriđ de eo . Ode 7 Vluriꝯ
tenueꝛ . 7 libi fueꝛ . Tra . ē . vi . caꝛ . In dñio . ē una . 7 x . uiłłi 7 i . ſeru
cū . iii . caꝛ . Ibi moliñ de . xii . deñ . 7 xvi . ac̄ p̄ti . Silua . i . leúu
lḡ . 7 iii . q̃ᵶ laꝵ . Valet . l . ſoliđ.
Iſd . R . ten in *MVLEWICHE* . iii . partes uniꝰ hidæ 7 Osb̄n de eo.
Suain 7 Rafuuin tenueꝛ . 7 libi fueꝛ . Tra . ē . iiii . caꝛ . In dñio
ē una . 7 iiii . uiłłi 7 iiii . borđ cū . iii . caꝛ . Ibi . i . ac̄ p̄ti . Silua una
leúu lḡ . 7 dim laꝵ . Valet . xx . ſoliđ.
Iſd . R . ten in *TICHESHALE* . iii . partes . i . hidæ . 7 Hugoǀ . 7 Alriꝯ
7 Orm̦ar tenueꝛ . 7 libi fueꝛ . Tra . ē . vi . caꝛ . In dñio . ē una . 7 iii.
ſerui . 7 vii . uiłłi 7 ii . borđ cū . ii . caꝛ . Ibi . vi . ac̄ p̄ti . Silua . i . leúu
lḡ . 7 iii . q̃rent laꝵ . Valet . xxx . ſoliđ.
Iſd . R . ten in *GESTREON* . iii . hiđ . 7 Hugo de eo . Goduiñ 7 Widegrip
tenueꝛ 7 libi fueꝛ . Tra . ē . iiii . caꝛ . Ibi ſunt ! ix . uiłłi 7 ii . borđ cū . ii.
caꝛ . Ibi . ix . ac̄ p̄ti . 7 de una parte molini . x . deñ . Silua dimiđ leúu
lḡ . 7 una q̃rent . laꝵ . Vał . xv . ſoliđ.
Iſd . R . ten in *TITESOVRE* . iii . hiđ . 7 Stenulf de eo . Vluiet 7 Godric
tenueꝛ . 7 libi fueꝛ Tra . ē . iii . caꝛ . In dñio . ē dimiđ caꝛ . 7 viii . uiłłi 7 ii . borđ
7 uñ ſeru . cū . i . caꝛ 7 dimiđ . Ibi . iiii . ac̄ p̄ti . 7 moliñ de . viii . denaꝛ.
Silua . vi . q̃rent lḡ . 7 tñtđ laꝵ . Valet . xxx . ſoliđ.

Robert also holds *
in BRADELEY ½ hide. Tanio holds from him. Wulfgeat and Alfward
held it; they were free. Land for 4 ploughs. In lordship 1; 3 slaves;
   3 villagers and 6 smallholders with 2 ploughs.
   Meadow, 4 acres; woodland 2 leagues long and 1 wide.
Value 40s.

in COLTON 1 hide. Geoffrey holds from him. Oda and Wulfric
held it; they were free. Land for 6 ploughs. In lordship 1;
   10 villagers and 1 slave with 3 ploughs.
   A mill at 12d; meadow, 16 acres; woodland 1 league long
     and 3 furlongs wide.
Value 50s.

in MILWICH three parts of 1 hide. Osbern holds from him.
Swein and Rafwin held it; they were free. Land for 4 ploughs.
In lordship 1;
   4 villagers and 4 smallholders with 3 ploughs.
   Meadow, 1 acre; woodland 1 league long and ½ wide.
Value 20s.

in TIXALL three parts of 1 hide. Hugh holds from him.
Alric and Ordmer held it; they were free. Land for 6 ploughs.
In lordship 1; 3 slaves;
   7 villagers and 2 smallholders with 2 ploughs.
   Meadow, 6 acres; woodland 1 league long and 3 furlongs wide.
Value 30s.

in INGESTRE 3 hides. Hugh holds from him. Godwin and Wilgrip *
held it; they were free. Land for 4 ploughs.
   9 villagers and 2 smallholders with 2 ploughs.
   Meadow, 9 acres; from one part of a mill, 10d;
     woodland ½ league long and 1 furlong wide.
Value 15s.

in TITTENSOR 3 hides. Stenulf holds from him. Wulfgeat
and Godric held it; they were free. Land for 3 ploughs.
In lordship ½ plough;
   8 villagers, 2 smallholders and 1 slave with 1½ ploughs.
   Meadow, 4 acres; a mill at 8d; woodland 6 furlongs long
     and as wide.
Value 30s.

Ipſe.R.ten in WESTONE.unā v̄ træ.7 Ernulf de eo.Vluricus
tenuit.Tra.e̅. .car.Ibi funt.v.uilli cū.ii.car.Silua.i.leuu
lḡ.7 dimid leuu lat.Valet.x.ſolid. IN TATEMANESLAV HD.

Ipſe.R.ten in CROTEWICHE unā v̄ træ.7 Vlfac de eo.Goding
tenuit.7 lib hō fuit.Tra.e̅.iiii.car.Ibi funt.iiii.uilli 7 iiii.bord
7 un feruus cū.iii.car.Ibi molin de.iiii.ſol.7 una ac pti.Silua
dimid leuu lḡ.7 dimid lat.Valet.xxiiii.ſolid.

Ipſe.R.ten in CAVRESWELLE.i.virg træ.7 Ernulf de eo.
Vluiet tenuit.7 lib hō fuit.Tra.e̅.iiii.car.In dnio.e̅ una.
7 x.uilli 7 ii.bord cū.iii.car.Ibi.vi.ac pti.7 Silua.i.leuu
lḡ.7 dimid lat.7 medietas æcclæ de Stoche cū dim caruc træ
Valet.xxx.ſolid.

Ipſe.R.ten in MADELIE dimid hid.7 Vlfac de eo.Hanc tenuit
Godiua etiā p aduentū regis.W.in anglia.fed recedere n̄ po
terat cū tra.Tra.e̅.vi.car.In dnio.e̅ una.7 v.ferui.7 x.uilli.
7 viii.bord.cū.iii.car.Ibi.ii.ac pti.Silua.i.leuu lḡ.7 iiii.
qrent lat.

In ead uilla de ead tra ten duo angli.i caruc træ 7 dimid.
7 ibi hnt.v.bord 7 ii.uillos cū.i.car.

Tot CO ualet.iiii.lib.

Ipſe.R.ten in BRANSELLE.unā v̄ træ.cuj v̄ medietas.e̅
regis ſic uia ea diuidit.fed.R.eand parte regis inuafit   .A.
7 fe defenfore facit.Bagod ten de eo.Vluiet tenuit.7 lib
hō fuit.Tra.e̅.iii.car.In dnio.e̅ una.7 ii.ferui.Ibi funt
.iiii.uilli 7 i.bord cū.i.car.Silua dimid leuu lḡ.7 iiii.qrent
lat.Valet.xx.ſolid.

Robert himself holds*
[in TOTMONSLOW Hundred] *
in WESTON (COYNEY) 1 virgate of land. Arnulf of Hesdin holds
from him. Wulfric held it. Land for 3 ploughs.
    5 villagers with 2 ploughs.
    Woodland 1 league long and ½ league wide.
Value 10s.

in TOTMONSLOW Hundred
in GRATWICH 1 virgate of land. Wulfheah holds from him.
Goding held it; he was a free man. Land for 3 ploughs.
    4 villagers, 4 smallholders and 1 slave with 3 ploughs.
    A mill at 4s; meadow, 1 acre; woodland ½ league long
        and ½ wide.
Value 24s.

in CAVERSWALL 1 virgate of land. Arnulf holds from him.
Wulfgeat held it; he was a free man. Land for 4 ploughs.
In lordship 1;
    10 villagers and 2 smallholders with 3 ploughs.
    Meadow, 6 acres; woodland 1 league long and ½ wide;
        a half of Stoke(-on-Trent) Church, with ½ carucate of land.*
Value 30s.

in MADELEY (HOLME) ½ hide. Wulfheah holds from him. Godiva held it
even after King William's arrival in England, but she could not
withdraw with her land. Land for 6 ploughs. In lordship 1;
5 slaves;
    10 villagers and 8 smallholders with 3 ploughs.
    Meadow, 2 acres; woodland 1 league long and 4 furlongs wide.
    In the same village 2 Englishmen hold 1½ carucates of this
        land; they have 5 smallholders and 2 villagers with 1 plough.
Value of whole manor £4.

in BRAMSHALL 1 virgate of land. A half of this virgate is
the King's, as the road divides it; but Robert has annexed   .A.*
the King's part and makes himself answerable.
Bagot holds from him. Wulfgeat held it; he was a free man.
Land for 3 ploughs. In lordship 1; 2 slaves;
    4 villagers and 1 smallholder with 1 plough.
    Woodland ½ league long and 4 furlongs wide.
Value 20s.

Ipſe.R.ten in ELACHESTONE .unā v̄ træ.7 Wodeman 7 Alſi
de eo.Sex taini tenueɍ.T.R.E.7 libi hões fueɍ.Tra.ē.vɪ.caɍ.
In dñio.ē una 7 dim caɍ.cū.ɪ.ſeruo.7 xɪ.uiłłi 7 ɪɪɪɪ.borð
cū.ɪ.caɍ 7 dimið.Ibi.xɪɪ. aͣc p̄ti.7 moliň de;xxxɪɪ.denaɼ
Silua.ɪ.leůu lḡ. 7 dimið laɍ.Valet.xxx.ſolið.

Ipſe.R.ten in BLORA.ɪ.virg træ.7 Edric de eo;Quattuor
teini tenueɍ.7 libi hões fueɍ.Tra.ē.v.caɍ.In dñio.ē.ɪ.caɍ.
7 ɪɪ.uiłłi cū.ɪ.caɍ.Ibi.ɪɪ.q̄rent Spineti.Val;v.ſolið.

Ipſe.R.ten in DVLVERNE unā v̄ træ.7 Walbͣt de eo.
Goduin tenuit.7 lib hõ fuit.cū.ɪɪ.aliis ſimiliͭ libis.Tra.ē
.ɪɪɪɪ.caɍ.In dñio.ē dimið caɍ.7 v.uiłłi 7 v.borð cū.ɪɪɪ,caɍ
7 dimið.Ibi.ɪ.aͣc p̄ti.Silua.ɪ.leůu lḡ.7 dimið laɍ.Val;xx.ſoł;

Ipſe.R.ten in CELLE.unā v̄ træ.7 Robͣt de eo.Godeua tenuit
7 liba fuit.Tra.ē.ɪɪɪɪ.caɍ.In dñio.ē una.7 vɪɪ.uiłłi 7 ɪ.borð
cū.ɪ.caɍ 7 dimið.Ibi moliň de.xɪɪ.deň.7 una aͨc p̄ti.Silua
ɪɪ.leůu lḡ.7 una laɍ.Valet.xx.ſolið. IN SAISDONE HVND;

Ipſe.R.ten in BVBINTONE.v.hið.7 Helgot de eo.Wifare
tenuit.cū ſaca 7 ſoca.Tra.ē.vɪ.caɍ.In dñio ſunt.ɪɪ;caɍ.7 ɪɪɪɪ;
ſerui.7 v.uiłłi 7 ɪɪɪ.borð cū.ɪ.caɍ.Silua paſtił.ɪ.leůu lḡ;
7 dimið laɍ.Valet.xʟ.ſolið.

Ipſe ten in PECLESHELLA.ɪɪɪ.hið.7 Hugo de eo.Brodor
tenuit.cū ſaca 7 ſoca.7 lib hõ fuit.Tra.ē.vɪ.caɍ.In dñio
ſunt.ɪɪ.caɍ.cū.ɪ.ſeruo.7 xɪɪ.uiłłi 7 vɪ.borð cū.ɪɪɪɪ.caɍ.Ibi
moliň de.xɪɪ.denaɍ.Silua dimið leůu lḡ.7 ɪɪɪɪ.q̄rent laɍ.
Valet.xxx.ſolið.

39 in **ELLASTONE** 1 virgate of land. Woodman and Alfsi hold from
him. 6 thanes held it before 1066; they were free men.
Land for 6 ploughs. In lordship 1½ ploughs, with 1 slave;
    11 villagers and 4 smallholders with 1½ ploughs.
    Meadow, 12 acres; a mill at 32d; woodland 1 league long
       and ½ wide.
Value 30s.

40 in **BLORE** 1 virgate of land. Edric holds from him. 4 thanes held it;
they were free men. Land for 5 ploughs. In lordship 1 plough;
    2 villagers with 1 plough.
    Spinney, 2 furlongs.
Value 5s.

41 in **DILHORNE** 1 virgate of land. Walbert holds from him.
Godwin held it; he was a free man; together with two others
likewise free. Land for 4 ploughs. In lordship ½ plough;
    5 villagers and 5 smallholders with 3½ ploughs.
    Meadow, 1 acre; woodland 1 league long and ½ wide.
Value 20s.

42 in **CHEADLE** 1 virgate of land. Robert holds from him.
Godiva held it; she was free. Land for 4 ploughs. In lordship 1;
    7 villagers and 1 smallholder with 1½ ploughs.
    A mill at 12d; meadow, 1 acre; woodland 2 leagues long
       and 1 wide.
Value 20s.

in **SEISDON** Hundred

43 in **BOBBINGTON** 5 hides. Helgot holds from him. Wivar held it,
with full jurisdiction. Land for 6 ploughs.
In lordship 2 ploughs; 4 slaves;
    5 villagers and 3 smallholders with 1 plough.
    Woodland pasture 1 league long and ½ wide.
Value 40s.

44 in **PATSHULL** 3 hides. Hugh holds from him. Broder held it,
with full jurisdiction; he was a free man. Land for 6 ploughs.
In lordship 2 ploughs, with 1 slave;
    12 villagers and 6 smallholders with 4 ploughs.
    A mill at 12d; woodland ½ league long and 4 furlongs wide.
Value 30s.

Ipſe.R.teñ in *ACHE* . v . hiđ.7 Hugo de eo . Brodor tenuit
7 liƀ hõ fuit. Tra . ē . iii . caſ . In dñio . ē una.7 iiii . uiłłi 7 iiii.
borđ cũ . i . caſ 7 dimiđ . Silua dimiđ leuu Ig.7 ii . q̃rent lat.
Valet . viii . ſoliđ.

Ipſe.R.teñ in *WROTOLEI* . ii . hiđ.7 Glodoen de eo. Hunta
tenuit.7 liƀ hõ fuit. Tra.ē. ii . caſ.In dñio.ē una.7 i . uiłłs 7 i . borđ.
Silua dimiđ leuu Ig.7 ii . q̃rent lat . Valet.iiii.ſoliđ.

Ipſe.R.teñ in *ACLE* . ii . hiđ.7 Helio de eo. Vluuiñ tenuit
7 liƀ hõ fuit. Tra . ē . iiii . caſ. In dñio. ē una.7 ii . uiłłi 7 vi . borđ
cũ . i . caſ.Ibi . iiii . aͨ p̃ti . Valet . xx . ſoliđ.

Ipſe.R.teñ in *FRICESCOTE* .ıı.hidas. .7 Turchil de eo . Quattuor teini
tenueſ.H̃ tra fuit c̃ſuetudinaria ſolũm de theloneo regis.
ſed aliã ſocã habeƀ.7 quo uoleƀ ire cũ tris poteraɴ . Ibi poſ
eͤ . caſ. In dñio . ē una caſ.7 ii . uiłłi cũ . i . caſ.7 duo angli
h̃nt ibi . i . caſ 7 dimiđ cũ . i . ſeruo . Valet.xvi . ſoliđ.

Ipſe.R.teñ in *WICENORE* . ii . hiđ.7 Roƀt de eo. Quattuor
teini tenueſ.7 liƀi fueſ . Tra . ē . iiii . caſ . In dñio . ē una caſ
7 iiii . uiłłi 7 ii . borđ.Ibi molĩ de . xviii . denaſ.Ibi.xx . aͨ
p̃ti . Silua dimiđ leuu Ig.7 v . q̃rent lat . Valet . xv . ſoliđ.

249 c

Iſđ . R . teñ in *RIDEWARE* . iii . v træ.7 Herman de eo . Treſ
taini tenueſ.7 liƀi h̃oͤs fueſ.Tra.ē . iiii . caſ.In dñio . ē una.
cũ . i . ſeruo.Ibi uñ liƀ hõ teñ unã v de hac tra.7 ibi h̃
ii . uiłł cũ dimiđ caſ.Ibi molĩ de . ii . ſoliđ.7 viii . aͨ p̃ti.
Silua . i . leuu Ig 7 dim.7 in lat . i . leuu . Valet . xv . ſoliđ.

45 in OAKEN 5 hides. Hugh holds from him. Broder held it;
he was a free man. Land for 3 ploughs. In lordship 1;
    4 villagers and 4 smallholders with 1½ ploughs.
    Woodland ½ league long and 2 furlongs wide.
Value 8s.

46 in WROTTESLEY 2 hides. Clodoen holds from him. Hunta held it;
he was a free man. Land for 2 ploughs. In lordship 1;
    1 villager and 1 smallholder.
    Woodland ½ league long and 2 furlongs wide.
Value 4s.

[in OFFLOW Hundred]
47 in OAKLEY 2 hides. Helio holds from him. Wulfwin held it;
he was a free man. Land for 4 ploughs. In lordship 1;
    2 villagers and 6 smallholders with 1 plough.
    Meadow, 4 acres.
Value 20s.

48 in SYRESCOTE 2 hides. Thorkell holds from him. 4 thanes
held it. This land was only (liable) for customary payment
of the King's toll; but they had a different jurisdiction, and
they could go with their lands wherever they would.
... ploughs possible. In lordship 1 plough;
    2 villagers with 1 plough; 2 Englishmen have 1½ ploughs,
      with 1 slave.
Value 16s.

49 in WICHNOR 2 hides. Robert holds from him. 4 thanes held it;
they were free. Land for 4 ploughs. In lordship 1 plough;
    4 villagers and 2 smallholders.
    A mill at 18d; meadow, 20 acres; woodland ½ league long
      and 5 furlongs wide.
Value 15s.

50 Robert also holds 3 virgates of land in (HAMSTALL) RIDWARE.   249c
Herman holds from him. 3 thanes held it; they were free men.
Land for 4 ploughs. In lordship 1, with 1 slave. A free man
holds 1 virgate of this land; he has
    2 villagers with ½ plough.
    A mill at 2s; meadow, 8 acres; woodland 1½ leagues long
      and in width 1 league.
Value 15s.

Ipſe . R . ten . ii . hid 7 Vrfer de eo.   IN CVDVLVESTAN HD.

Vluric tenuit 7 lib hō fuit . Tra . ē . ii . car .7 vii . uilli .7 v . bord
cū . ii . car . Ibi moliñ de xii . deñ .7 una quarent ſiluæ.

7 Valet . xvi . ſolid.

Ipſe . R . ten in HALTONE . iii . hid .7 Vrfer de eo . Vluric tenuit.
Tra . ē . iiii . car . In dñio ſunt . ii . car cū . i . ſeruo .7 vi . uilli
7 vii . bord cū . iii . car . Ibi . vi . ac p̄ti . Silua . i . q̄rent lg
7 dimid q̄rent lat . Valet . xxx . ſolid.

Ipſe . R . ten in LEVINTONE dimid hid .7 Giſlebt de eo.
Ailric 7 Ormar tenuer .7 libi fuer . Tra . ē . i . car . Vaſta . ē

Ipſe . R . ten in WILBRESTONE . iii . hid . Val . ii . ſolid.
7 Laurenti de eo . Tres taini tenuer .7 libi fuer . Tra . ē . v . car
In dñio ſunt . ii . car .7 ii . ſerui .7 ii . uilli 7 iii . bord cū . i . car.
Ibi . iii . ac p̄ti . Silua dimid leuu lg .7 tntd lat . Val . xv.

Ipſe . R . ten in BRVNITONE . ii . hid .7 Warin de eo . ſolid.
Quinq; teini tenuer .7 libi fuer . Tra . ē . iii . car . Ibi ſuƴ
iii . uilli 7 ii . bord cū . ii . car . Ibi . viii . ac p̄ti . Silua . ii.
quarent lg .7 tntd lat . Valet . x . ſolid.

Ipſe . R . ten in BRVMHELLE . i . hida . Warin de eo . Quinq;
frs tenuer .7 libi fuer . Tra . ē . iiii . car . In dñio . ē una
cū . i . ſeruo .7 vii . uilli 7 iiii . bord cū . vi . car . Ibi . ii . ac
p̄ti . Silua . i . leuu lg .7 una q̄rent lat.

In Ruſcote . ē una hida p̄tin ad eund m̄ . Tot ual . xx . ſol.

Robert himself holds *
51 in CUTTLESTONE Hundred 2 hides. Urfer holds from him. Wulfric
held it; he was a free man. Land for 2 ploughs;
    7 villagers and 5 smallholders with 2 ploughs.
    A mill at 12d; 1 furlong of woodland.
Value 16s.

52 in HAUGHTON 3 hides. Urfer holds from him. Wulfric, a free man,
held it. Land for 4 ploughs. In lordship 2 ploughs, with 1 slave;
    6 villagers and 7 smallholders with 3 ploughs.
    Meadow, 6 acres; woodland 1 furlong long and ½ furlong wide.
Value 30s.

53 in LOYNTON ½ hide. Gilbert holds from him. Alric and Ordmer
held it; they were free. Land for 1 plough. Waste.
Value 2s.

54 in WILBRIGHTON 3 hides. Lawrence holds from him. 3 thanes held it;
they were free. Land for 5 ploughs. In lordship 2 ploughs; 2 slaves;
    2 villagers and 3 smallholders with 1 plough.
    Meadow, 3 acres; woodland ½ league long and as wide.
Value 15s.

55 in BRINETON 2 hides. Warin holds from him. 5 thanes held it;
they were free. Land for 3 ploughs.
    3 villagers and 2 smallholders with 2 ploughs.
    Meadow, 8 acres; woodland 2 furlongs long and as wide.
Value 10s.

56 in BLYMHILL 1 hide. Warin holds from him. 5 brothers held it;
they were free. Land for 4 ploughs. In lordship 1, with 1 slave;
    7 villagers and 4 smallholders with 6 ploughs.
    Meadow, 2 acres; woodland 1 league long and 1 furlong wide.
In Brockhurst 1 hide, which belongs to this manor.
Value of the whole 20s.

Ipſe.R.teñ in *ESTRETONE*.iii.hiđ.7 Herueus de eo.
Tres teini tenueŕ 7 libi fueŕ.Tra.ē.vi.caŕ.In dñio.ē
una.7 iiii.uitti.7 viii.borđ cū.i.caŕ.Ibi uñ miles teñ
unā caruc træ.7 hŕ ibi.i.caŕ.Ibi moliñ de.iiii.ſoł.
7 vi.ac pti.Silua hŕ dim leuu lḡ.7 iii.q̃rent laŕ.
Valet.xvi.foliđ.

Ipſe.R.teñ in *ETONE*.i.hidā.7 Herueus de eo.Ordmeŕ
tenuit 7 lib fuit.Tra.ē.iii.caŕ.In dñio.ē una caŕ.
7 iii.ſerui.7 iii.uitti 7 iiii.borđ cu.i.caŕ.Ibi moliñ
de.iii.foliđ.Valet.viii.ſoł.

Ipſe.R.teñ in *GRAGELIE*.i.hiđ.7 Herueus de eo.Bodin
tenuit 7 lib hō fuit.Tra.ē.ii.caŕ.Ibi.ē uñ uitts.
7 una ac pti.Valet.ii.foliđ.

Ipſe.R.teñ in *ORRETONE*.i.hiđ.7 Clodoan de eo.
Æilric tenuit 7 lib hō fuit.Tra.ē.ii.caŕ.In dñio eſt
una.7 ii.ſerui.7 ii.borđ cū.i.caŕ.Valet.iii.foliđ.

Ipſe.R.teñ in *SARDONE*.ii.hiđ.7 Herueus de eo.
Quattuor teini libi tenueŕ.Tra.ē.ii.caŕ.In dñio
eſt una.cū.i.ſeruo.7 ii.uitti 7 iiii.borđ cū.i.caŕ.
Valet.v.foliđ.

Ipſe.R.teñ in *COVE*.i.hiđ.7 Bueređ de eo.Ælric
tenuit.7 lib fuit.Tra.ē.ii.caŕ.In dñio.ē una.7 iiii.
ſerui.7 ii.uitti 7 ii.borđ cū.i.caŕ.Ibi.iii.ac pti.
Silua dimiđ leuu lḡ.7 una q̃rent laŕ.In dñio
regis.ē Ħ ſilua.   Tra.ualet.xvi.foliđ.

Ipſe.R.teñ in *COPEHALE*.i.hiđ.7 Bueret de eo.Tres libi
hōes tenueŕ.Tra.ē.iiii.caŕ.In dñio.ē una.7 viii.uitti
7 vi.borđ cū.iii.caŕ.Valet.xii.foliđ.

57 in STRETTON 3 hides. Hervey holds from him. 3 thanes
held it; they were free. Land for 6 ploughs. In lordship 1;
    4 villagers and 8 smallholders with 1 plough.
    1 man-at-arms holds 1 carucate of land; he has 1 plough.
    A mill at 4s; meadow, 6 acres; woodland ½ league long
      and 3 furlongs wide.
Value 16s.

58 in (WATER) EATON 1 hide. Hervey holds from him. Ordmer held it;
he was free. Land for 3 ploughs. In lordship 1 plough; 3 slaves;
    3 villagers and 4 smallholders with 1 plough.
    A mill at 3s.
Value 8s.

59 in GAILEY 1 hide. Hervey holds from him. Bodin held it;
he was a free man. Land for 2 ploughs.
    1 villager.
    Meadow, 1 acre.
Value 2s.

60 in OTHERTON 1 hide. Clodoen holds from him. Alric held it;
he was a free man. Land for 2 ploughs. In lordship 1; 2 slaves;
    2 smallholders with 1 plough.
Value 3s.

61 in (GREAT) SAREDON 2 hides. Hervey holds from him. 4 free
thanes held them. Land for 2 ploughs. In lordship 1, with 1 slave;
    2 villagers and 4 smallholders with 1 plough.
Value 5s.

62 in COVEN 1 hide. Burgred holds from him. Alric held it;
he was free. Land for 2 ploughs. In lordship 1; 4 slaves;
    2 villagers and 2 smallholders with 1 plough.
    Meadow, 3 acres; woodland ½ league long and 1 furlong wide;
      this woodland is in the King's lordship.
Value of the land 16s.

63 in COPPENHALL 1 hide. Burgred holds from him. Three free men
held it. Land for 4 ploughs. In lordship 1;
    8 villagers and 6 smallholders with 3 ploughs.
Value 12s.

Ipſe . R . ten in *Serveſed* 7 Herucus de eo . Duo libi

hões tenueř . Tra . ē . iii . cař . Ibi ſunt . ii . uiłłi 7 v . borđ

cū . i . cař . Silua dimiđ leūu lg̅ . 7 dim lať . Valet . x . ſol.

Ipſe . R . ten in *Eitone* . iii . hiđ . 7 Godric de eo . Wilegrip

tenuit ut lib hō . Tra . ē . vii . cař . In dñio . ē una . 7 iii . ſerui.

7 viii . uiłłi 7 viii . borđ cū p̄bro hñt . iii . cař . Ibi . iiii . ac̅

p̄ti . Silua . i . q̅rent lg̅ . 7 tñtđ lať . Valet . xx . ſolid.

249 d

Ipſe . R . ten in *Levehale* . iii . hiđ . 7 Briend 7 Drogo de eb̄

Tres libi hões tenueř . Tra . ē . vii . cař . In dñio . ē una

cař . 7 v . uiłłi 7 ii . borđ cū . i . ſeruo hñt . iii . cař . Ibi . ii . ac̅

p̄ti . Valet . x . ſoliđ.

Ipſe . R . ten in *Ricardeſcote* . ii . hiđ 7 dim . 7 Robt

de eo . Eduin tenuit . 7 jacet ad Bradelie . Tra . ē . iiii . cař.

In dñio . ē una . 7 iii . uiłłi 7 iii . borđ cū . i . cař . Ibi . ii . ac̅

p̄ti . Valet . xx . ſoliđ.

Ipſe . R . ten in *Monetvile* . i . hidā . 7 Walter 7 Anſger

de eo . Eduin tenuit . Tra . ē . ii . cař . In dñio ſuÿ ibi cū . viii .

borđ . Ibi . ii . ac̅ p̄ti . Valet . x . ſoliđ.

.XII. **WTERRA Willi Filij Anscvlfi. *In Saisdon Hvnd.***

Willelm . F . Anſculfi ten de rege *Segleslei*.

Algar tenuit . Ibi . vi . hidæ . Tra . ē . xii . cař.

In dñio . ē una cař . 7 iii . ſerui . 7 xlv . uiłłi cū p̄bro 7 ii . borđ

hñt . xviii . cař . Ibi xvi . ac̅ p̄ti . Silua . ii . leūu lg̅ . 7 una

lať . T.R.E. ualb . x . lib . Modo ſimilit.

Parte̅ ſiluæ huj Ꝏ . calūniant p̄bri de hantone.

249 c, d

64 in SHARESHILL 3 hides. Hervey holds from him. Two free men held them. Land for 3 ploughs.
2 villagers and 5 smallholders with 1 plough.
Woodland ½ league long and ½ wide.
Value 10s.

65 in (CHURCH) EATON 3 hides. Godric holds from him. Wilgrip held it as a free man. Land for 7 ploughs. In lordship 1; 3 slaves.
8 villagers and 8 smallholders with a priest have 3 ploughs.
Meadow, 4 acres; woodland 1 furlong long and as wide.
Value 20s.

249 d

66 in LEVEDALE 3 hides. Bryant and Drogo hold from him. 3 free men held it. Land for 7 ploughs. In lordship 1 plough.
5 villagers and 2 smallholders with 1 slave have 3 ploughs.
Meadow, 2 acres.
Value 10s.

67 in RICKERSCOTE 2½ hides. Robert holds from him. Earl Edwin held it; it lies in (the lands of) Bradley. Land for 4 ploughs. In lordship 1;
3 villagers and 3 smallholders with 1 plough.
Meadow, 2 acres.
Value 20s.

68 in MONETVILE 1 hide. Walter and Ansger hold from him. Earl Edwin held it. Land for 2 ploughs. They are there, in lordship, with
8 smallholders.
Meadow, 2 acres.
Value 10s.

2   LAND OF WILLIAM SON OF ANSCULF

In SEISDON Hundred
1 William son of Ansculf holds SEDGLEY from the King. Earl Algar held it. 6 hides. Land for 12 ploughs. In lordship 1 plough; 3 slaves.
45 villagers with a priest and 2 smallholders have 18 ploughs.
Meadow, 16 acres; woodland 2 leagues long and 1 wide.
Value before 1066 £10; now the same.
The priests of Wolverhampton claim part of the woodland of this manor.

Iſd.W.teñ _MORVE_.Ibi.v.hidæ.Tra.ē.vi.cař.Vaſta.ē.

Tres libi hões tenueř.T.R.E. Silua Longit hŧ.ii.leuu 7 tñtđ lat.

Iſd.W.teñ in _CATSPELLE_.i.hiđ.Tra.ē.ii.cař.In foreſta

regis eſt.7 uaſta.ē.

Iſd.W.teñ in _SEGLESLEI_.ii.hiđ.7 Goisfriđ de eo.7 ibi hŧ.i.cař

in dñio.7 ix.uiłł cū.ii.cař.7 ii.aĉs p̃ti.Valet.xx.ſoł.

Iſd.W.teñ in _PENNE_.iii.hiđ.7 Giſlebŧ de eo.Godeua comitiſſa

tenuit.Tra.ē.vi.cař.In dñio.ē una.7 vi.uiłłi cū.i.libo

hōē hñt.i.cař 7 dimiđ.Ibi.iiii.aĉ p̃ti.Valet.xx.ſoliđ.

Iſd.W.teñ in _PENNE_.v.hiđ.7 Robŧ de eo.Algar te

nuit.Tra.ē.vi.cař.In dñio.ē una.cū.i.ſeruo.7 viii.uiłłi

7 ii.borđ cū.i.cař.Ibi moliñ de.ii.ſoliđ.Valuit.7 uał.xxx.ſoł.

Iſd.W.teñ in _OVERTONE_.iii hiđ.7 Walbŧ de eo.Vltan

tenuit 7 liŧ hō fuit.Tra.ē.iiii.cař.In dñio ſunt.ii.7 ii.ſerui.

7 vii.uiłłi 7 ii.borđ cū.ii.cař.Ibi.iiii.aĉ p̃ti.

Valuit 7 uał.xl.ſoliđ.

Iſd.W.teñ in _WAMBVRNE_.vii.hiđ.7 Radulf de eo.

Turſtiñ tenuit cū ſaca 7 ſoca.Tra.ē.viii.cař.In dñio

ſunt.ii.7 viii.ſerui. 7 xiiii.uiłłi cū pbro 7 iii.borđ

hñt.iiii.cař.Ibi.ii. molini de.iiii.ſoliđ.7 iiii.aĉ p̃ti.

Valuit 7 ualet.iii.liŧ.

Iſd.W.teñ in _OXELIE_.i.hiđ.7 Robŧ de eo.Goduiñ 7 Alric

tenueř.7 libi fueř.Tra.ē.ii.cař.In dñio.ē una.7 iiii.uiłłi

cū.i.cař.Ibi.ii.aĉ p̃ti.Valuit 7 uał.xv.ſoliđ.

William also holds*

2   MORFE 5 hides. Land for 6 ploughs. Waste. 3 free men
held it before 1066.
    The woodland has 2 leagues length and as much width.

3   in CHASEPOOL 1 hide. Land for 2 ploughs. In the King's Forest; waste.

4   in SEDGLEY 2 hides. Geoffrey holds from him. He has 1 plough
in lordship;
    9 villagers with 2 ploughs.
    Meadow, 2 acres.
Value 20s.

5   in (LOWER) PENN 3 hides. Gilbert holds from him. Countess Godiva
held them. Land for 6 ploughs. In lordship 1.
    6 villagers with 1 free man have 1½ ploughs.
    Meadow, 4 acres.
Value 20s.

6   in (UPPER) PENN 5 hides. Robert holds from him. Earl Algar
held it. Land for 6 ploughs. In lordship 1, with 1 slave;
    8 villagers and 2 smallholders with 1 plough.
    A mill at 2s.
The value was and is 30s.

7   in ORTON 3 hides. Walbert holds from him. Wulfstan held it;
he was a free man. Land for 4 ploughs. In lordship 2; 2 slaves;
    7 villagers and 2 smallholders with 2 ploughs.
    Meadow, 4 acres.
The value was and is 40s.

8   in WOMBOURN 7 hides. Ralph holds from him. Thurstan held it, with
full jurisdiction. Land for 8 ploughs. In lordship 2; 8 slaves.
    14 villagers with a priest and 3 smallholders have 4 ploughs.
    2 mills at 4s; meadow, 4 acres.
The value was and is £3.

9   in OXLEY 1 hide. Robert holds from him. Godwin and Alric
held it; they were free. Land for 2 ploughs. In lordship 1;
    4 villagers with 1 plough.
    Meadow, 2 acres.
The value was and is 15s.

Ipſe.W.ten̄ in *EFNEFELD*.iii.hiđ.7 Giſleƀt de eo.Alric̄ tenuit
cū ſoca.tein̄ regis.E.Tra.ē.iiii.caŕ.In dn̄io.ē una cū.i.ſeruo.
7 v.uiłłi 7 i.borđ hn̄t.i.caŕ 7 dim.Ibi.iiii.ac̄ p̄ti.Silua.i.leuu
lḡ.7 dimiđ laŕ.Rex ten̄ eā in foreſta.Valuit 7 uał.xxℓiiii.ſoł.
Iſđ.W.ten̄ in *CIPPEMORE*.iii.hiđ.7 Roger de eo.Eduin̄
tenuit ut liƀ hō.Tra.ē.iiii.caŕ.In dn̄io ſunt.ii.7 iii.ſerui.
7 v.borđ.Silua.i.leuu in lḡ 7 laŕ.Rex h̄t in foreſta.
Valuit 7 uał.x.ſoliđ.
Iſđ.W.ten̄ in *HIMELEI*.ii.hiđ dimiđ v træ min̄.7 Arni de eo.
Vltan 7 Rauechetel tenueŕ.7 liƀi fueŕ.Tra.ē.iii.caŕ.In dn̄io
eſt una.7 viii.uiłłi 7.iii.borđ cū.ii.caŕ.Ibi.ii.ac̄ p̄ti.7 Silua.
Valuit 7 uał.xxiiii.ſoliđ.
In eađ uilla ten̄ Giſleƀt de Wiłło.i.hiđ.Luuet tenuit.7 liƀ
hō fuit.Tra.ē.ii.caŕ.In dn̄io.ē una.7 iii.uiłłi 7 ii.borđ cū.i.caŕ.
Ibi.i.ac̄ p̄ti.Valuit 7 uał.x.ſoliđ.
Iſđ.W.ten̄ in *ELMELECOTE*.i.hiđ.7 Pagen de eo.Duo hōes
comitis
Algari tenueŕ.ſine ſoca.Tra.ē.ii.caŕ.Ibi ſunt.iiii.uiłłi 7 ii.borđ
7 un ſeru cū.ii.caŕ.Ibi.iiii.ac̄ p̄ti.7 Silua.
Valuit 7 uał.x.ſoliđ.

Ipſe.W.ten̄ in *TRESLEI*.ii.hiđ.7 Balduin de eo.Turgot
tenuit cū ſaca 7 ſoca.7 liƀ hō fuit.Tra.ē.iii.caŕ.In dn̄io ſunt
ii.caŕ.7 v.ſerui.7 iiii.uiłłi 7 i.borđ cū.ii.car.Ibi molin̄ de
iiii.ſoliđ.7 iiii.ac̄ p̄ti.
Valuit 7 uał.xxx.ſoliđ.

0 William holds 3 hides in ENVILLE himself. Gilbert holds from him.
  Alric, a thane of King Edward's, held it, with the jurisdiction.
  Land for 4 ploughs. In lordship 1, with 1 slave.
    5 villagers and 1 smallholder have 1½ ploughs.
    Meadow, 4 acres; woodland 1 league long and ½ wide; the
      King holds it, in the Forest.
  The value was and is 24s.
    William also holds*
1 in CIPPEMORE 3 hides. Roger holds from him. Edwin held it
   as a free man. Land for 4 ploughs. In lordship 2; 3 slaves;
     5 smallholders.
     Woodland 1 league in length and width; the King has it,
       in the Forest.
   The value was and is 10s.

2 in HIMLEY 2 hides less ½ virgate of land. Arni holds from
   him. Wulfstan and Ravenkel held it; they were free.
   Land for 3 ploughs. In lordship 1;
     8 villagers and 3 smallholders with 2 ploughs.
     Meadow, 2 acres; a woodland.*
   The value was and is 24s.

3 In the same village Gilbert holds 1 hide from William.
   Lovett held it; he was a free man. Land for 2 ploughs.
   In lordship 1;
     3 villagers and 2 smallholders with 1 plough.
     Meadow, 1 acre.
   The value was and is 10s.

4 William also holds 1 hide in AMBLECOTE. Payne holds from
   him. Two of Earl Algar's men held it, without jurisdiction.
   Land for 2 ploughs.
     4 villagers, 2 smallholders and 1 slave with 2 ploughs.
     Meadow, 4 acres; a woodland.*
   The value was and is 10s.

5 William holds 2 hides himself in TRYSULL, and Baldwin from   250 a
   him. Thorgot held it, with full jurisdiction; he was a free
   man. Land for 3 ploughs. In lordship 2 ploughs; 5 slaves;
     4 villagers and 1 smallholder with 2 ploughs.
     A mill at 4s; meadow, 4 acres.
   The value was and is 30s.

Ipſe.W.ten in Cocortone .1.hid 7 dimid.7 Balduin de eo.
Tres libi hões tenuer.ſed ſoca erat regis.Tra.ē.11.car.Vaſta.ē.
Ipſe.W.ten in Seisdone.v.hid.7 Walbt de eo.Quatuor
libi hões tenuer.ſed ſoca eoᵹ regis erat.Tra.ē.vi.car.
In dnio.ē una.7 ibi ſunt.11.ſeruientes.7 Ibi.1111.ac p̄ti.
Valuit 7 ual.v111.ſolid.
Iid.W.ten in Etinghale.11.hid 7 Robᵗ de eo.Turſtan
tenuit cū ſaca 7 ſoca.Tra.ē.1111.car.In dnio ſunt.ii.7 ix.
uiłłi 7 111.bord cū.11.car.Ibi.v.ac p̄ti.Silua hɫ.111.q̄rent
in łg 7 lat.Valuit 7 ual.xxx.ſolid.
Iſd.W.ten in Biscopesberie.11.hid 7 11.v 7 dimid.7 Robt
de eo.Vlfric tenuit cū ſaca 7 ſoca.Tra.ē.v.car.Ibi ſunt
111.uiłłi 7 1111.bord cū.11.car.Ibi.vi.ac p̄ti.
Valuit 7 ual.xx.ſolid.
Iſd.W.ten in Pendeford.11.hid.7 Almar de eo.Vlſtan
7 Goduin tenuer.7 libi hões fuer.Tra.ē.111.car.In dnio.ē
una.7 111.ſerui.7 1111.uiłłi 7 v.bord.cū.1.car.Ibi.1111.ac p̄ti.
Valuit 7 ual xx.ſolid.
Iſd.W.ten in Moleslei.1.hidā.7 Rogeri de eo.Godeua comitiſſa
tenuit.Tra.ē.11.car.In dnio.ē una.7 un uiłłs 7 11.bord
cū.1.car.7 ibi.1.ac p̄ti.Silua.11.q̄rent łg.7 una lat.
Valuit 7 ual.v111.ſolid.   In Cvdvlvestan hd.
Rogeri ten de.W.11.hid træ in Eseningetone.
Tra.ē.vi.car.In dnio.ē una.7 11.ſerui.7 xv.uiłłi cū.11.
bord hnt.111.car.Silua.1.leu łg.7 tntd lat.In Biſcopeſ
berie.ē una v træ p̄tin huic Ꝏ.ſᷓ uaſta.ē omino.

6 William holds 1½ hides himself in 'CROCKINGTON', and Baldwin
from him. 3 free men held it, but the jurisdiction
was the King's. Land for 2 ploughs. Waste.

7 William holds 5 hides himself in SEISDON, and Walbert from
him. 4 free men held it, but their jurisdiction was the
King's. Land for 6 ploughs. In lordship 1;
   2 Servants.*
   Meadow, 4 acres.
The value was and is 8s.

  William also holds*

8 in ETTINGSHALL 2 hides. Robert holds from him. Thurstan
held it, with full jurisdiction. Land for 4 ploughs. In lordship 2;
   9 villagers and 3 smallholders with 2 ploughs.
   Meadow, 5 acres; the woodland has 3 furlongs in length and width.
The value was and is 30s.

9 in BUSHBURY 2 hides and 2½ virgates. Robert holds from him.
Wulfric held it, with full jurisdiction. Land for 5 ploughs;
   3 villagers and 4 smallholders with 2 ploughs.
   Meadow, 6 acres.
The value was and is 20s.

:0 in PENDEFORD 2 hides. Aelmer holds from him. Wulfstan and
Godwin held it; they were free men. Land for 3 ploughs.
In lordship 1; 3 slaves;
   4 villagers and 5 smallholders with 1 plough.
   Meadow, 4 acres.
The value was and is 20s.

1 in MOSELEY 1 hide. Roger holds from him. Countess Godiva
held it. Land for 2 ploughs. In lordship 1;
   1 villager and 2 smallholders with 1 plough.
   Meadow, 1 acre; woodland 2 furlongs long and 1 wide.
The value was and is 8s.

  In CUTTLESTONE Hundred

2 Roger holds 2 hides of land from William in ESSINGTON.
Land for 6 ploughs. In lordship 1; 2 slaves.
   15 villagers with 2 smallholders have 3 ploughs.
   Woodland 1 league long and as wide.
   In BUSHBURY is 1 virgate of land which belongs to
     this manor, but it is altogether waste.

Valuit 7 ualet.xx.ſoliđ.Godeua comitiſſa tenuit.

Walƀtus teñ de.W.i.hiđ in *Bradeleg. In Offelav* Hđ.

Tra.ē.ii.caŕ.Ibi.iiii.uiłłi hñt.i.caŕ.Silua.iii.q̃ʒ lḡ.

7 una q̃ʒ laꝉ.Valuit 7 uaꝉ.lxiiii.denaŕ.Vntan tenuiꞇ.

cū ſaca 7 ſoca.Ibi.ii.aꞓ p̃ti.

Roƀt teñ de.W.iii.hiđ in *Alrewic*.Tra.ē.iii.caŕ.

In dñio ſꞇ.ii.cū.i.ſeruo.7 v.uiłłi cū.i.borđ hñt.ii.caŕ.

Ibi.i.aꞓ p̃ti.7 Silua paſtiꝉ.v.q̃ʒ lḡ.7 iii.q̃ʒ laꝉ.ƒ habeƀ.

Valuit 7 uaꝉ.xv.ſoliđ.Duo taini liƀe tenueꝛ.7 rex ſocā

Iđē teñ de.W.iiiʴ.hiđ in *Barra*.Tra.ē.iii.caŕ.Ibi nil

ē in dñio.ſed tanꝓ.i.uiłłs ibi.ē cū.i.borđ.

Silua paſtiꝉ.i.leu lḡ.7 iiii.q̃rent laꝓ.Valuit 7 uaꝉ.v.ſoꝉ.

Turchil teñ de.W.i.hiđ in *Rischale*.ƒ Waga tenuit.

Tra.ē.ii.caŕ.In dñio.ē dim̃ caŕ.7 vi.uiłłi cū.ii.borđ

hñt.i.caŕ 7 dim̃.Ibi moliñ de.iiii.deñ.7 una aꞓ p̃ti.

Silua paſtiꝉ.v.q̃ʒ lḡ.7 ii.q̃ʒ laꝉ.Valuit 7 uaꝉ.x.ſoliđ.

Wiuara tenuit cū ſaca 7 ſoca.

Drogo teñ de.W.iii.hiđ in *pirio*.Tra.ē.iii.caŕ.In dñio

ē una caŕ.7 iiii.uiłłi 7 iii.borđ ſꞇ ibi.Ibi moliñ de xvi.deñ.

Ibi.iiii.aꞓ p̃ti.Silua.i.leu lḡ.7 dim̃ leu laꝉ.Valuit 7 uaꝉ

xx.ſoliđ.Luuare tenuit cū ſaca 7 ſoca.

The value was and is 20s.
  Countess Godiva held it.

In OFFLOW Hundred
23 Walbert holds 1 hide from William in BRADLEY.
  Land for 2 ploughs.
    4 villagers have 1 plough.
    Woodland 3 furlongs long and 1 furlong wide.
  The value was and is 64d.
    Untan held it, with full jurisdiction.
    Meadow, 2 acres.

24 Robert holds 3 hides from William in ALDRIDGE.
  Land for 3 ploughs. In lordship 2, with 1 slave.
    5 villagers with 1 smallholder have 2 ploughs.
    Meadow, 1 acre; woodland pasture 5 furlongs long
      and 3 furlongs wide.
  The value was and is 15s.
    2 thanes held it freely. The King had the jurisdiction.

25 He also holds 3 hides from William in (GREAT) BARR.
  Land for 3 ploughs. Nothing in lordship, but only
    1 villager there, with 1 smallholder.
    Woodland pasture 1 league long and 4 furlongs wide.
  The value was and is 5s.
    Waga held it.

26 Thorkell holds 1 hide from William in RUSHALL.
  Land for 2 ploughs. In lordship ½ plough;
    6 villagers with 2 smallholders have 1½ ploughs.
    A mill at 4d; meadow, 1 acre; woodland pasture 5 furlongs
      long and 2 furlongs wide.
  The value was and is 10s.
    Wivar held it, with full jurisdiction.

27 Drogo holds 3 hides from William in PERRY (BARR).
  Land for 3 ploughs. In lordship 1 plough;
    4 villagers and 3 smallholders.
    A mill at 16d; meadow, 4 acres; woodland 1 league long
      and ½ league wide.
  The value was and is 20s.
    Leofwara held it, with full jurisdiction.

Idē teñ de.W.iii.hiđ in *BARRE*.Tra.ē.iii.car.In dñio
eſt una.7 ii.uilli cū.i.borđ hñt.i.car.Ibi.i.ac̃ p̃ti.Silua
iiii.q̃rent lḡ.7 tñtđ lat.Valuit 7 ual.v.ſoliđ.
Alured tenuit cū ſaca 7 ſoca.

250 b

Idē Drogo teñ de.W.i.hiđ in *HONESWORDE*.
Tra.ē.ii.car.In dñio.ē una.7 vi.uilli cū.iiii.lc̃.đ
hñt.ii.car.Ibi moliñ de.ii.ſol.7 ii.ac̃ p̃ti.Silua
dimiđ leū lḡ.7 tñtđ lat.Valuit 7 ual.xx.ſoliđ.
Ailuerd 7 Aluuiñ tenuer̃ cū ſaca 7 ſoca.

Willelm filius Corbucion tenet.x.hiđ in *SIBEFORD*.
7 Radulfus de eo.Tra.ē.vii.car.In dñio.ē una.
7 ii.ſerui.7 vi.uilli cū.iii.car.Ibi moliñ.xxxii.deñ.7 iiii.
ac̃ p̃ti.Paſtura.vii.q̃ẓ lḡ 7 lat.Valuit 7 ual.iiii.lib.

Tvrstiñ tenet.v.hiđ in *DRAITON*.Tra.v.car.In dñio
.iii.car.7 ii.ſerui.7 xii.uilli 7 iiii.borđ cū.iii.car.Ibi mđ
linū.iiii.ſolidoẓ.Valuit.c.ſoliđ.modo.viii.lib.

250 c

.XIII. **TERRA RICARDI FOREST** *IN PEREHOLLE HD.*
Ricard Foreſtari teñ de rege *TVRVOLDESFELD*.7 Nigel
de eo.Bernuʼf tenuit 7 lib hō fuit.Ibi.ē.i.virg tre.Tra.ē
ii.car.Ibi.ē una cū.ii.uillis 7 i.borđ.Silua.i.leuu lḡ.7 tñtđ
lat.Valet.x.ſoliđ.
Iſđ.R.teñ Witemore.7 Nigel de eo.Vlfac tenuit 7 lib hō fuit.
Ibi.ē dimiđ hida.Tra.ē.iii.car.In dñio.ē una.7 iii.uilli
7 ii.borđ cū.i.car.Ibi.i.ac̃ p̃ti.Silua.i.leuu lḡ.7 dim lat.
Valet.x.ſoliđ.

28 He also holds 3 hides from William in (GREAT?) BARR.
Land for 3 ploughs. In lordship 1;
    2 villagers with 1 smallholder have 1 plough.
    Meadow, 1 acre; woodland 4 furlongs long and as wide.
The value was and is 5s.
    Alfred held it, with full jurisdiction.

29 Drogo also holds 1 hide from William in HANDSWORTH.   250 b
Land for 2 ploughs. In lordship 1;
    6 villagers with 4 smallholders have 2 ploughs.
    A mill at 2s; meadow, 2 acres; woodland ½ league long
       and as wide.
The value was and is 20s.
    Alfward and Alwin held it, with full jurisdiction.

30 William son of Corbucion holds 10 hides in SIBFORD,* and Ralph
from him. Land for 7 ploughs. In lordship 1; 2 slaves;
    6 villagers with 3 ploughs.
    A mill at 32d; meadow, 4 acres; pasture 7 furlongs long
       and wide.
The value was and is £4.

31 Thurstan holds 5 hides in DRAYTON*. Land for 5 ploughs.
In lordship 3 ploughs; 2 slaves;
    12 villagers and 4 smallholders with 3 ploughs.
    A mill at 4s.
The value was 100s; now £8.

13   LAND OF RICHARD FORESTER   250 c

In PIREHILL Hundred
1 Richard Forester holds THURSFIELD from the King, and Nigel
from him. Bernwulf held it; he was a free man. 1 virgate
of land. Land for 2 ploughs; 1 there, with
    2 villagers and 1 smallholder.
    Woodland 1 league long and as wide.
Value 10s.

Richard also holds*
2 WHITMORE. Nigel holds from him. Wulfheah held it; he was a
free man. ½ hide. Land for 3 ploughs. In lordship 1;
    3 villagers and 2 smallholders with 1 plough.
    Meadow, 1 acre; woodland 1 league long and ½ wide.
Value 10s.

Iſd.R.teñ NORMANESCOTE .7 Almar 7 Vluric de eo . Vlmar
tenuit.7 lib hō fuit.Ibi.1.virg træ.Tra.ē.1.car.In dñio.ē una.
Silua.111.qrent lg.7 11.qrent lat.Valet.11.ſol.

Iſd.R.teñ HENEFORD .7 Nigell de eo.Ibi.ē una v træ.Tra
ē.1.car.Vaſta.ē.Toulf tenuit.Silua modica xx.ptic in lg
7 lat.Valet.11.ſolid.

Iſd.R.teñ HANCESE .Pata tenuit.7 lib hō fuit.Ibi ſunt
.111.partes dimid hidæ.Tra.ē.11.car.Ibi ſunt.11.uilti 7 v11.bord
cū.1.car 7 dimid.7 Ibi.1.ac pti.Silua.11.qz lg.7 una lat.
Valet.v.ſolid.

Iſd.R.teñ CLAITONE .7 Nigel de eo.Sagrim tenuit 7 lib
hō fuit.Ibi.ē dimid hida.Tra.ē.111.car.In dñio.ē dimid
car.7 1111.uilti 7 v1.bord cū.1.car 7 dimid.Silua ibi.1.leu
lg.7 dimid lat.Valet.x.ſolid.

Iſd.R.teñ in DVLMESDENE .unā v træ.Gladuin 7 Goduin
tenuer 7 libi fuer.Tra.ē.11.car.Ibi ſunt.v.uilti 7 11.bord
cū.11.car.7 1111.ac pti.Silua.x11.qrent lg.7 v1.lat.
Valet.x.ſolid.

Iſd.R.teñ CLOTONE .Goduin tenuit 7 lib hō fuit.Ibi.ē una
virg træ.Tra.ē.11.car.Ibi ſunt.1111.uilti cū.1.bord hñt
unā car.7 1111.ac pti.Valet: v..ſolid. IN CVLVESTAN HD.
Iſd.R.teñ in REDBALDESTONE .111.hid.Tra.ē.111.car.
Alli tenuit 7 lib hō fuit.In dñio.ē una car.cū.1111.bord.
Valuit.11.ſolid.Modo.xv.ſolid.

Iſd.R.teñ in ESTENDONE .unā hid vaſtam.

3 NORMACOT. Aelmer and Wulfric hold from him. Wulfmer held it;
he was a free man. 1 virgate of land. Land for 1 plough.
In lordship 1.
Woodland 3 furlongs long and 2 furlongs wide.
Value 2s.

4 HANFORD. Nigel holds from him. 1 virgate of land. Land for 1 plough.
Waste. Tholf held it.
A small wood 20 perches in length and width.
Value 2s.

5 HANCHURCH. Pata held it; he was a free man. Three parts of
half a hide. Land for 2 ploughs.
2 villagers and 7 smallholders with 1½ ploughs.
Meadow, 1 acre; woodland 2 furlongs long and 1 wide.
Value 5s.

6 CLAYTON. Nigel holds from him. Saegrim held it; he was a
free man. ½ hide. Land for 3 ploughs. In lordship ½ plough;
4 villagers and 6 smallholders with 1½ ploughs.
Woodland 1 league long and ½ wide.
Value 10s.

7 in DIMSDALE 1 virgate of land. Gladwin and Godwin held it;
they were free. Land for 2 ploughs.
5 villagers and 2 smallholders with 2 ploughs.
Meadow, 4 acres; woodland 12 furlongs long and 6 wide.
Value 10s.

*8 KNUTTON. Godwin held it; he was a free man. 1 virgate of land.
Land for 2 ploughs.
4 villagers with 1 smallholder have 1 plough.
Meadow, 4 acres.
Value 5s.

In CUTTLESTONE Hundred

9 in RODBASTON 3 hides. Land for 3 ploughs. Alli held it;
he was a free man. In lordship 1 plough, with
4 smallholders.
The value was 2s; now 15s.

10 in HUNTINGTON 1 hide. Waste.

XII. **R**ainaldi Bailgiole. *In Colvestan Hvnd.*

Rainald de Balgiole ten de rege . iiii . hid in *Westone*
7 *Bertone* 7 *Brotone* . Noue teini tenuer T.R.E . p . ix . m̃.
Ibi fuer . xi . car . Tra . e . vi . car . In dnio funt . iii . car . 7 ii.
ſerui . 7 x . uilli cu . ii . car . Silua harū trarū ht . i . leuu lḡ.
7 dimid leu lat . Valet . xl . ſolid.
De hac tra ten Amerland de Raẏnaldo . i . hid . Ibi ht . iii.
feruos 7 i . bord . Valet . v . folid.   *In Pereholle Hvnd.*
Iſd Rainald ten *Niwetone* . Goduia tenuit . 7 lib hō fuit . Ibi . e
dimid hida . Tra . e . iiii . car . In dnio . e dimid car . 7 viii . uilli 7 v.
bord cu . iii . car . Ibi . i . feruus . 7 moliñ de . iiii . folid . 7 ii . ac pti . Silua
una qrent lḡ . 7 una lat . Valet . xl . folid . *In Tateslav Hvnd.*

.XV. **R**advlfi filij Hvberti.

Radvlf . F . Hubti ten de rege in *Bretlei* . ii . hid . 7 Robt⁹ de buci
de eo . Leuric tenuit . 7 lib hō fuit . Tra . e . iii . car . In dnio
eſt una . 7 vi . uilli 7 iiii . bord cu . ii . car . Ibi . i . ac pti.
Silua . i . leuu lḡ . 7 dimid lat . Valuit . v . fol . Modo . x . fol.
Iſd Robt⁹ ten in *Chingeslei* . i . hid . 7 Nigel de eo . Leuric
tenuit 7 lib hō fuit . Tra . e . i . car . Ipfa . e in dnio . 7 ii . ac pti.
Silua ibi . i . leuu lḡ . 7 iiii . qq lat . Valuit . vi . fol . m . x . fol.

4   LAND OF REGINALD BALLIOL

In CUTTLESTONE Hundred
1 Reginald of Balliol holds from the King 4 hides in WESTON (-under-
   Lizard) and BEIGHTERTON and BROCKTON (GRANGE). 9 thanes held
   them before 1066 as 9 manors. There were 11 ploughs.
   Land for 6 ploughs. In lordship 3 ploughs; 2 slaves;
       10 villagers with 2 ploughs.
       The woodland of these lands has 1 league length
           and ½ league width.
   Value 40s.
       Amerland holds 1 hide of this land from Reginald. He has
       3 slaves and 1 smallholder. Value 5s.

In PIREHILL Hundred
2 Reginald also holds NEWTON. Godwin held it; he was a free
   man. ½ hide. Land for 4 ploughs. In lordship ½ plough;
       8 villagers and 5 smallholders with 3 ploughs; 1 slave.
       A mill at 4s; meadow, 2 acres; woodland 1 furlong
           long and 1 wide.'
   Value 40s.

5   LAND OF RALPH SON OF HUBERT

In TOTMONSLOW Hundred
1 Ralph son of Hubert holds 2 hides from the King in BRADLEY
   (-in-the-Moors). Robert of Bucy holds from him. Leofric held it;
   he was a free man. Land for 3 ploughs. In lordship 1;
       6 villagers and 4 smallholders with 2 ploughs.
       Meadow, 1 acre; woodland 1 league long and ½ wide.
   The value was 5s; now 10s.

2 Robert of Bucy also holds 1 hide from Ralph in KINGSLEY, and
   Nigel from him. Leofric held it; he was a free man.
   Land for 1 plough; it is in lordship.
       Meadow, 2 acres; woodland 1 league long and 4 furlongs wide.
   The value was 6s; now 10s.

.XVI. **N**̄TERRA NIGELLI.

IGELLVS ten̄ *TORP* . Ibi funt . III . hidæ . T́ra . ē . vi . caŕ.

In dñio . ē una . 7 vII . uilti 7 vi . borđ hūt . IIII . caŕ.

Ibi . vIII . ãc p̃ti . Valuit xx̄ . fot . Modo . xL . fot . Vluuin̄ tenuit.

Hanc t́rā calūniat́ Nicolaus ad firmā regis in Cliftone.

250 d

.XVII **C**̄TERRA TAINOᵶ REGIS. *IN SEIESDON HVND*:

HENVIN tenet de rege in *CODESHALE* . III . hiđ . Ipfe tenuit

T.R.E. T́ra . ē . III . caŕ . Ibi funt . vi . uilti cū . II . caŕ.

VDI ten̄ de rege . I . hiđ . in *SERESDONE* . Gamel tenuit . fᵶ foᴇa ej̄

fuit regis . T́ra . ē . II . caŕ . Ibi funt . III . uilti cū . I . caŕ . 7 una ãc p̃ti:

ALRIC ten̄ de rege in *BIGEFORD* . III . virǵ t́ræ . Ipfe tenuit . T.Ŕ.E:

7 liƀ hō fuit . T́ra . ē . I . caŕ.

Hi . III . hōes redđt uicecom̄ . xII . fot p̄ fingulos annos.

ALVRIC̨ ten̄ in *CHENET* . I . caruc t́ræ . Tra . ē . I . caŕ:

Ibi hī . III . borđ . 7 ual . v . foliđ.

ALMARVS ten̄ in *BISPESTONE* . I . caruc t́ræ . Ernui tenuit . 7 liƀ

hō fuit . T́ra . ē . I . caŕ . Ibi . ē in dñio . c̨ū . II . borđ . Ibi . III . ãc p̃ti.

Valet . II . foliđ.   *IN PEREHOLLE HVND*:

DVNNING ten̄ *CHENISTETONE* . 7 ipfe tenuit T.R.E.

T́ra . ē . I . caŕ . Ipfa ibi . ē cū . II . feruis . 7 dimiđ ãc p̃ti . Silua . II . q̃ᵶ

lḡ . 7 II . q̃ᵶ lī . Valet . II . foliđ.

LEVING ten̄ *MOCLESTONE* . Alric 7 Edric tenueŕ T.R.E. Ibi eſt

6   LAND OF NIGEL*

[In OFFLOW Hundred]

1   Nigel holds THORPE (CONSTANTINE). 3 hides. Land for 6 ploughs.
In lordship 1.
     7 villagers and 6 smallholders have 4 ploughs.
     Meadow, 8 acres.
     The value was 20s; now 40s.
     Wulfwin held it. Nicholas claims this land for the King's
revenue in Clifton (Campville).

(16, 2-3 are entered after 17,21, at the foot of col. 250 d, opposite 16,1)

7   LAND OF THE KING'S THANES   250 d

In SEISDON Hundred

1   Kenwin holds 3 hides from the King in CODSALL. He held it himself
before 1066. Land for 3 ploughs.
     6 villagers with 2 ploughs.

[In CUTTLESTONE Hundred]

2   Udi holds 1 hide from the King in [LITTLE] SAREDON. Gamel held it,
but its jurisdiction was the King's. Land for 2 ploughs.
     3 villagers with 1 plough.
     Meadow, 1 acre.

3   Alric holds 3 virgates of land from the King in BICKFORD. He held
it himself before 1066; he was a free man. Land for 1 plough.

4   These three men pay the Sheriff 12s a year.*

5   Aelfric holds 1 carucate of land in CANNOCK. Land for 1 plough. He has
     3 smallholders.
     Value 5s.

[In PIREHILL Hundred]*

6   Aelmer holds 1 carucate of land in BISHTON. Ernwy held it;
he was a free man. Land for 1 plough. It is in lordship, with
     2 smallholders.
     Meadow, 3 acres.
     Value 2s.

In PIREHILL Hundred.

7   Dunning holds KNIGHTON; he held it himself before 1066.
     Land for 1 plough. It is there, with 2 slaves.
     Meadow, ½ acre; woodland 2 furlongs long and 2 furlongs wide.
     Value 2s.

8   Leofing holds MUCKLESTONE. Alric and Edric held it before 1066. 1 hide.
     Land for 3 ploughs.

una hida.Tra.e̅.iii.car.Ibi p̄br 7 iii.uiłłi hn̅t.i.car.Ibi.i.ac̄
p̄ti.Silua.ii.q̊ᶻ lg̅.7 tn̄td lat.Valet.v.solid.

Isd̄ Leuing ten̄ WENNITONE.Ibi.e̅ una v trӕ.Tra.e̅.i.car.
Ibi sunt.ii.uiłłi cu̅.i.bord.7 dim ac̄ p̄ti.Silua.iii.q̊rent lg̅.
7 ii.q̊ᶻ lat.Valet.ii.solid.

VLVVIN ten̄ BETELEGE.Godric 7 Vluiet tenuer̅ 7 liƀi fuer̅.
Ibi.e̅ dimid hida.Tra.i.car.Ibi.e̅ ipsa cu̅.ii.uiłłis 7 uno bord
Ibi.i.ac̄ p̄ti.Silua.i.leuu lg̅.7 dimid lat.Valet.iiii.solid.

Isd̄ Wluin ten̄ BALTREDELEGE.Goduin tenuit 7 liƀ ho̅ fuit.
Ibi dimid v trӕ.Tra.e̅.i.car.Ibi sunt.ii.uiłłi cu̅.i.bord.7 dim
ac̄ p̄ti.Silua.i.leuu lg̅.7 dim lat.Valet.iiii.solid.

GAMEL ten̄ de rege BALTREDELEGE.Vluric tenuit.
Ibi dimid v trӕ.Tra.e̅.ii.car.Ibi.e̅ un uiłłs cu̅.iii.bord 7 dimid
car.7 dimid ac̄ p̄ti.Silua.vi.q̊ᶻ lg̅.7 iii.q̊ᶻ lat.Vał.iiii.soł.

Isd̄ Gamel ten̄ ALDIDELEGE.Vluric 7 Godric tenuer̅ 7 liƀi fuer̅.
Ibi dimid hida.Tra.e̅.iii.car.In dn̅io.e̅ una car.7 iiii.uiłłi
7 iii.bord cu̅.i.car.Ibi.i.ac̄ p̄ti.Silua.ii.leuu lg̅.7 una lat.
Valet.x.solid.

Isd̄ Gamel ten̄ TALC.Godric tenuit 7 liƀ ho̅ fuit.Ibi.e̅.una v
trӕ.Tra.e̅.i.car.Ipsa.e̅ ibi cu̅.iiii.uiłłis.7 una ac̄ p̄ti.
Silua.i.leuu lg̅.7 tn̄td lat.Valet.iii.solid.

SPERRI ten̄ WESTONE.Vlfelm tenuit.Ibi.e̅ dimid v trӕ.
Tra.e̅.i.car.Ibi.e̅ un uiłłs 7 iii.ac̄ p̄ti.Valet.ii.solid.

A priest and 3 villagers have 1 plough.
Meadow, 1 acre; woodland 2 furlongs long and as wide.
Value 5s.

9 Leofing also holds WINNINGTON. 1 virgate of land.
Land for 1 plough.
2 villagers with 1 smallholder.
Meadow, ½ acre; woodland 3 furlongs long and 2 furlongs wide.
Value 2s.

0 Wulfwin holds BETLEY. Godric and Wulfgeat held it; they were
free. ½ hide. Land for 1 plough. It is there, with
2 villagers and 1 smallholder.
Meadow, 1 acre; woodland 1 league long and ½ wide.
Value 4s.

1 Wulfwin also holds BALTERLEY. Godwin held it; he was
a free man. ½ virgate of land. Land for 1 plough.
2 villagers with 1 smallholder.
Meadow, ½ acre; woodland 1 league long and ½ wide.
Value 4s.

2 Gamel holds BALTERLEY from the King. Wulfric held it. ½ virgate
of land. Land for 2 ploughs.
1 villager with 3 smallholders and ½ plough.
Meadow, ½ acre; woodland 6 furlongs long and 3 furlongs wide.
Value 4s.

3 Gamel also holds AUDLEY. Wulfric and Godric held it; they were
free. ½ hide. Land for 3 ploughs. In lordship 1 plough;
4 villagers and 3 smallholders with 1 plough.
Meadow, 1 acre; woodland 2 leagues long and 1 wide.
Value 10s.

4 Gamel also holds TALKE. Godric held it; he was a free
man. 1 virgate of land. Land for 1 plough. It is there, with
4 villagers.
Meadow, 1 acre; woodland 1 league long and as wide.
Value 3s.

5 Sperri holds WESTON (-upon-Trent). Wulfhelm held it. ½ virgate of
land. Land for 1 plough.
1 villager.
Meadow, 3 acres.
Value 2s.

R<small>ICARD</small> ten A*NNE* . Ailric tenuit.Ibi.ē dim hida.Tra.ē.ii.car.

A<small>LRICVS</small> ten S*TAGRIGESHOLLE* . Ipſe tenuit 7 lib hō fuit.
Ibi.ii.car.7 una v træ.Ibi ſunt.ii.uilli 7 v.bord cū.i.car.
7 ii.ac p̄ti.Silua.xl.ptic lḡ.7 tntd lat.Valet.v.ſolid.

A<small>LWOLD</small> ten C*ROCHESDENE* .Ipſe tenuit T.R.E.7 lib hō fuit.
Ibi.ē dimid v træ.Tra.ē.ii.car.In dñio.ē dimid car.7 iiii.
bord hñt.i.car.Ibi.i.ac p̄ti.Valet.v.ſolid.

O<small>THA</small> ten C*EDLA* .Vluiet tenuit.Ibi.ē dim hida.Tra.ē
iii.car 7 dimid.In dñio.ē dimid car.7 iii.uilli
Ibi.ii.ac p̄ti.Silua.i.leūu lḡ.7 tntd lat.Valet.v.ſolid

L<small>EVILD</small> ten S*CEOTESTAN* .Ibi.ē dim hida. I*N* C*VDOLVESTAN* HD.
Tra ē.iii.car.Ibi.iii.uilli cū.i.bord hñt dim car.Ibi.ii.ac p̄ti.

A<small>LWARD</small> ten F*ENTONE* .Ibi.ē una v træ.   Vat.iiii.ſot.
Tra.ē.iii.car.Waſta.ē.

I<small>DE</small> Nigell ten de rege|.iii.hid.Tra.ē.iii.car.Leuric libe tenuit T.R.E.
Ibi ſt.iiii.uilli 7 vii.bord cū.i.car 7 dim.7 una ac p̄ti.
    De ipſa tra ten Liolf.ii.hid de Nigello.Tot uat.xvii.ſolid.
I<small>DE</small>.N.ten.i.hid in M*ORTONE* .Tra.ii.car.Wlfric libe tenuit T.R.E.
Ibi.ē in dñio.i.car.7 ii.uilli 7 ii.bord cū.i.car.Valet.x.ſolid.

250 d

[In CUTTLESTONE Hundred]
16 Richard holds (LITTLE) ONN. Alric held it. ½ hide.
Land for 2 ploughs.

[In TOTMONSLOW Hundred]
17 Alric holds STRAMSHALL. He held it himself; he was
a free man. 2 carucates and 1 virgate of land.
2 villagers and 5 smallholders with 1 plough.
Meadow, 2 acres; woodland 40 perches long and as wide.
Value 5s.

18 Alfwold holds CROXDEN. He held it himself before 1066; he was a free
man. ½ virgate of land. Land for 2 ploughs. In lordship ½ plough.
4 smallholders have 1 plough.
Meadow, 1 acre.
Value 5s.

19 Otto holds CHECKLEY. Wulfgeat held it. ½ hide.
Land for 3½ ploughs. In lordship ½ plough;
3 villagers.
Meadow, 2 acres; woodland 1 league long and as wide.
Value 5s.

In CUTTLESTONE Hundred
20 Leofhild holds SHUSHIONS. ½ hide. Land for 3 ploughs.
3 villagers with 1 smallholder have ½ plough.
Meadow, 2 acres.
Value 4s.

[In PIREHILL Hundred]
21 Alfward holds FENTON. 1 virgate of land. Land for 3 ploughs. Waste.

[16]   [LAND OF NIGEL] *

2 Nigel also holds 3 hides from the King in KINGSLEY.
Land for 3 ploughs. Leofric held it freely before 1066.
4 villagers and 7 smallholders with 1½ ploughs.
Meadow, 1 acre.
Ligulf holds 2 hides of this land from Nigel.
Total value 17s.

*3 Nigel also holds 1 hide in MORETON. Land for 2 ploughs. Wulfric
held it freely before 1066. In lordship 1 plough;
2 villagers and 2 smallholders with 1 plough.
Value 10s.

STAFFORDSHIRE HOLDINGS
ENTERED ELSEWHERE IN THE SURVEY*

DERBYSHIRE

3   LAND OF BURTON ABBEY   27?

[REPTON Wapentake]

ED   3 M. In WINSHILL the Abbot of Burton had 2 carucates of land taxable.
1   Land for 3 ploughs. Now in lordship 2 ploughs;
        10 villagers who have 1½ ploughs. King William placed
           there 6 Freemen who belong to Repton; they have 1 plough.
        1 mill, 5s 4d; meadow, 8 acres; underwood 1 league long
           and 1 furlong wide.
        Value before 1066, 20s; now 60s.

ED   5 M. In STAPENHILL the Abbot of Burton had 4 carucates and 2 bovates
2   of land taxable. Land for 4 ploughs. Now in lordship 2 ploughs;
        12 villagers who have 2 ploughs.
        Meadow, 4 acres; woodland pasture 1 league long
           and 3 furlongs wide.
        Value before 1066 and now, 60s.

6   LAND OF HENRY OF FERRERS   274 b

REPTON Wapentake

ED   14 M. In CROXALL Siward had 3 carucates of land taxable.
3   Land for 8 ploughs. Now in lordship 2 ploughs;
        35 villagers and 11 smallholders who have 8 ploughs.
        2 mills, 18s; meadow, 22 acres; underwood 2 furlongs long
           and 1 furlong wide.
        Value before 1066 £3; now £4.
        Roger holds it.

ED   15   In EDINGALE 1 carucate of land taxable. Land for 1 plough.
4   4 villagers have 1 plough.
        Underwood 3 furlongs long and 1 furlong wide.

14   LAND OF NIGEL OF STAFFORD   278 a

[REPTON Wapentake]

ED   2 M. In STAPENHILL Godric had 6 bovates of land taxable.
5   Land for 1 plough; now in lordship 1 plough.
        4 villagers and 3 smallholders have 1 plough.
        Meadow, 3 acres; underwood 1 furlong long and 1 wide.
        Value before 1066 and now 10s.

[REPTON Wapentake]

12 M. In EDINGALE Algar had 2 carucates of land taxable.
　　Land for 3 ploughs.
　　　12 villagers now have 8 ploughs.
　　　Meadow, 4 acres; underwood 3 furlongs long and 1 wide.
　　　Value before 1066 and now 40s.

CLIFTON CAMPVILLE. See 16,1 note.

RTHAMPTONSHIRE

16　　　　　　　LAND OF ST. REMY'S, RHEIMS　　　　　222 d

In CUTTLESTONE Hundred
1　St. Remy's Church holds LAPLEY from the King, and held it
　　likewise before 1066, With its dependencies, 3 hides.
　　Land for 6 ploughs. In lordship 3 ploughs; 5 slaves;
　　　18 villagers and 9 smallholders with 8 ploughs.
　　　Meadow, 16 acres; wood 3 furlongs long and as wide.
　　　Value 50s.

2　In MARSTON 2 of St. Remy's men hold 1 hide. Land for 1 plough.
　　Value 5s.
　　　Godwin held it, with full jurisdiction.

35　　　　　LAND OF WILLIAM SON OF ANSCULF　　　　　226 b

[In OFFLOW Hundred]
3　Ralph holds 3 hides from William in (WEST) BROMWICH.
　　Land for 3 ploughs. In lordship 1 ;
　　　10 villagers and 3 smallholders have 3 ploughs.
　　　Woodland 1 league long and ½ league wide.
　　The value is and was 40s.
　　　Brictwin held it.

IROPSHIRE

4　　　　　　　LAND OF EARL ROGER　　　　　257 b

14　**Land of William Pandolf**
In HODNETT Hundred
5　William also holds TYRLEY. Wulfric and Ravensward held it as 2
　　manors; they were free 1 hide paying tax. Land for 2 ploughs.
　　　4 villagers and 1 slave with 1 plough.
　　The value was 17s; now 20s.

EW 1

8   [In SEISDON Hundred]
Auti holds 3 hides in QUATT from the Earl.
Land for 12 ploughs. In lordship 4; 5 slaves;
    19 villagers and 14 smallholders with 10 ploughs.
    Meadow, 1 acre; woodland 2 leagues long and 1 wide;
       a mill at 2s.
The value was £6; now 100s.
    Auti also held it freely.

EW 2

9   Walter holds 1 hide in ROMSLEY from the Earl.
Land for 7 ploughs. In lordship 1; 2 slaves;
    7 villagers and 7 smallholders with 3 ploughs.
    Woodland 1 league long and ½ league wide.
The value was 30s; now 40s.
    Aki held it freely.

EW 3

10   Ralph holds 5 hides in RUDGE from the Earl.*
Land for 7 ploughs. In lordship 1, with 1 slave;
    3 villagers and 4 smallholders with 2 ploughs.
The value was 60s; now 40s.
    Edric held it freely from Earl Leofric.

EW 4

11   Ralph also holds 1 hide in SHIPLEY from the Earl. *
Land for 3 ploughs.
    2 villagers.
    Oaks, 1 furlong in length and width.
Value 5s.
    Alfsi held it freely before 1066.

EW 5

19   In CUTTLFSTONE Hundred
William also holds CHILLINGTON. 3 hides. Land for 6 ploughs.
In lordship 1 plough; 9 slaves;
    13 villagers and 6 smallholders with 5 ploughs.
    Meadow, 2 acres; woodland 2 leagues long and ½ league wide.
The value was £4; now 30s.
    The Bishop of Chester claims this land.

EW 6

27,6 is a duplicate of Staffs 12,22

WORCESTERSHIRE
    KINGSWINFORD, KINVER, see 1,27 note.

NOTES

ABBREVIATIONS used in the notes.

DB..Domesday Book. MS..Manuscript. EPNS..English Place-Name Society Survey.
VCH..Victoria County History, Staffs., vol.4 (1958). OEB..G. Tengvik *Old English
Bynames,* Uppsala 1938. PNDB..O. von Feilitzen *The Pre-Conquest Personal Names
of Domesday Book,* Uppsala 1937.

The manuscript is written on leaves, or folios, of parchment (sheep-skin), measuring about 15
inches by 11 (38 by 28 cm), on both sides. On each side, or page, are two columns, making
four to each folio. The folios were numbered in the 17th century, and the four columns of
each are here lettered a,b,c,d. The manuscript emphasises words and usually distinguishes
chapters and sections by the use of red ink. Underlining indicates deletion.

B 1   HONOUR. *Honor* equivalent to *feudum,* Holding; in DB, mainly, but not always, used
       for the Holdings of Earls and great magnates.
B 5   EARLDOM. *Comitatus,* normally used in DB for English 'Shire'; here in the continental
       sense of the holdings of a count or earl.
B 11   EACH YEAR. The only explicit statement that *geldum* was levied annually by 1086;
       though originally and formally imposed only in emergency, it had become virtually
       annual.
L 7   THE FIGURE is misplaced against Samson, instead of against the Wolverhampton
       Canons, as in the text. The text gives two chapters viii, misnumbering ix and x as
       viii and ix, but omitting the figure x.
1,1   KINGSWINFORD. See 1,27 note.
       'CROCKINGTON'. The name survives as a lane, between Trysull and Seisdon, VCH 38.
1,6   THE KING HOLDS. The words are repeated at the beginning of sections 6-32, but
       not 33-65.
1,7   WOODLAND. Here, and occasionally elsewhere, *ht i leug long,* 'has 1 league long'.
1,8   AND A REEVE. After *bord, h* was first written, evidently for *h(abe)nt,* have, and 7
       was written over the letter, presumably when the reeve was noticed.
1,9   OFFLOW. The Hundred heading has been inserted in the wrong place.
       TAMWORTH. The Borough is not entered in DB. Its burgesses are entered here, a mile
       to the north, with 8 more three miles to the south at Drayton Bassett (1,30), where
       they 'worked like other villagers', and 10 at Coleshill in Warwickshire (1,5..238b),
       nine miles to the south.
1,13   SANDON. See 11,10 note.
       WOODLAND. See 1,7 note.
1,20   WOODLAND. See 1,7 note.
1,25   WOODLAND. The letters *b* and *a* correct the word order.
1,27   KINVER. See also Worcestershire 1,4 'From KINVER 100s is paid, at 20d to the *ora* .
       This land is in Staffordshire. So also is Kingswinford. From this manor, and from two
       others in Worcestershire, that is Tardebigge, at 9 hides, and Clent, at 9 hides, from
       these three manors £15 of pence is paid to the Sheriff at 20 to the *ora*'.
       1,5 'TARDEBIGGE..9 hides..the Sheriff of Staffordshire receives and pays the
       revenue of this manor in Kingswinford.' 1,6 'CLENT..9 hides...the revenue of this
       manor, £4, is paid in Kingswinford in Staffordshire'. Both Worcestershire manors lie
       south-east of Kingswinford, 15 and 7 miles distant, all three on the line of a probable
       Roman road from Greensforge in Kingswinford to Alcester. They are grouped together
       at the end of the King's Worcestershire holdings, possibly because at one time they
       had all had the same holder.
1,33   PIREHILL. MS Cuttlestone, in error.
       IN. Repeated at the beginning of sections 33-47.
1,38   SHELTON. Under-Harley.
1,48   TOTMONSLOW. MS Pirehill, in error.
       IN. Repeated at the beginning of sections 48-64.
1,50   MUSDEN. The name is preserved by Musden Grange.
1,58   NEWTON. In Draycott-in-the-Moors.
       CARUCATES. Here, and in the two previous entries, the genitive, *terrae,* of land, is used
       to distinguish *car(ucatae)* from *car(ucae),* ploughs.

2,2   THE BISHOP HIMSELF HOLDS. Repeated at the beginning of sections 2-8 and 15-22.
2,3   R...HIDES. R for *require*, 'enquire' into (how many hides).
2,5   PIREHILL. The Hundred heading is inserted one line too early, presumably because no room was left in the following line.
2,6   R QT...HIDES. *R qt trae, (require quantum terrae),* 'enquire how much land'.
2,8   HIDES. Omitted, as in 2,3 and 2,6, but without marginal query.
2,11   IN. Repeated before each of the following place names.
'DORSLOW'. Near Sugnall; the name survived until the 16th century, VCH 42.
CHORLTON. Hill and Chapel Chorlton.
2,15   THE BISHOP...HOLDS. See 2,2 note.
2,20   WALTON. In Eccleshall.
2,22   HORTON. Near Tamhorn, perhaps in Fisherwick.
HARBORNE. A space equivalent to 4 or 5 letters is left before *terra* in the MS.
WILLIAM HOLDS IT. Either 'it', referring to Tipton, or 'them', referring to Smethwick and Tipton.
4,1   STAFFORD. Possibly in error for Burton, VCH 43, citing Staffordshire Historical Collections v (i) 3,7.
4,2   THE ABBEY...HOLDS. Repeated at the beginning of sections 2-10.
4,10   PILLATON. *Bedintona et Pilatehala* in the 12th century, VCH 44. Pillaton Hall survives.
7   CANONS OF WOLVERHAMPTON. The whole of this chapter is reproduced word for word in Heming's Cartulary (folio 189b, pp 430-433 ed. Hearne). The only variants are in 7,17, 3 villagers and 1 smallholder for 7 villagers, and in 7,18, 1 virgate for 3 virgates, and 3 smallholders for 4. Heming wrote at Worcester when Samson was its Bishop, and used contemporary returns. It is possible that his *iii villani* in 7,17 are a misreading of *vi*, giving 6 villagers and 1 smallholder for 7 villagers; in 7,18 the first stroke of the *iiii bordarii* in DB looks like an inserted correction.
SAMSON. Chaplain to King William, later Bishop of Worcester, 1096-1112. He was probably the editor, compiler, and writer of the Domesday Book (V.H. Galbraith in *English Historical Review*, 82, 1967, 86, and in *Domesday Book* (1975) 50, and 110).
7,16   CUTTLESTONE. The heading is unnecessarily repeated, since 7,13-18 were all in this Hundred. Heming read the entry as *'Ferdestan ... in Colvestan Hundredo'*.
8,2   THE EARL...HOLDS. Repeated at the beginning of 2-7, 10-15 and 17-28.
8,4   'CUBBINGTON'. *Cobintone* is possibly Cubbington in Warwickshire, near Leamington (6,7; 16,53; 20,1). It is not however listed in Earl Roger's Warwickshire lands, and the three Warwickshire entries between them constitute two 5 hide units. It might be a lost place in Staffordshire, though probably not Kibblestone.
REGINALD. Of Balliol.
8,5   ST. EVROUL'S. The historian Ordericus Vitalis was born and baptised at Atcham, by the Roman town of Wroxeter, east of Shrewsbury, and entered the monastery of St. Evroul, near Lisieux, in youth. The priest at Sheriff Hales, 13 miles east of Atcham, was the only dependent of the monastery in the locality, and may therefore have influenced the decision of Ordericus and his father to send the boy there.
EDWIN HELD. *Tenuerit* may be an error for *tenuerat*, or may be intended to mean that Edwin, Earl Algar's son, should have held the place, but did not.
8,10   THE EARL...HOLDS. Repeated at the beginning of 10-15 and 17-28, but not 16.
REGER. Perhaps in error for Roger, as in 8,11
8,15   19 ACRES. MS *xiiii* altered to *xvii*, with *ii* added above the line.
8,16   COLT. Probably Littlehay in Colton.
8,21   LAND FOR. The words *est terra* are partially erased; Farley omits them.
8,27   WOODLAND. See 1,7 note.
8,29   R. *require*, 'enquire' into the missing figure.
9   THE CHAPTER is misnumbered *VIII* in the MS.
10   THE CHAPTER is misnumbered IX in the MS, which has no chapter numbered X.
OFFLOW. MS, wrongly, Pirehill Hundred.
10,2   BURTON. *Burtone* might conceivably be an error for *Burg Tone*, the 'town' of the castle of Tutbury, VCH 48. But since the castle itself has already been distinguished from its surrounding *burgus* (as with other newly founded castles, e.g. Rhuddlan (Cheshire FT 2), Berkhamstead (Herts. B 11 note) and elsewhere, with varying terms for *burgus*), the description of a cultivated *tun*, 'village', around the castle walls, within the Borough, seems improbable. It is possible that Henry also had a castle at Burton-on-Trent, with the land entered in 10,10, or possibly at another Burton.
10,7   1 HIDE. The two half hides of 10,6 and 10,7.
10,10 BURTON. See 10,2 note.

11	ROBERT OF STAFFORD. Younger son of Roger of Tosny.
11,2	ROBERT...HOLDS. Repeated at the beginning of 2-6 and 8-17.
11,6	BRADLEY. By Stafford, see B 6.
	BURTON. In Castle Church.
11,7	KING'S PART. See B 12.
11,8	ROGER... HOLDS. Repeated at the beginning of 8-17.
11,10	'LITTLE SANDON'. No longer known as such. Since Cadio held it, it probably adjoined his Aston and Stoke holdings, north east of modern Sandon. Sandon may therefore be DB Little Sandon, and Sandon Hall the site of DB Sandon (1,13).
11,12	LEOFWIN. Bishop of Lichfield 1053-1067.
	THEM. *Has,* referring to the hides.
	AND 2. Presumably slaves, with the number of ploughs not stated.
11,14	WOODLAND. See 1,7 note.
11,23	ALGOT. Possibly identical with Helgot.
11,27	HILDERSTONE. The writing in this entry leaves a gap of a quarter of an inch, surrounding a beautifully executed contemporary repair to a cut. The gap occurs at *Heldvlves/tone, libi/hoes, bord/7 and dimid/lat,* and is matched by a similar gap on the other side of the repair, in 12,8.
11,28	ROBERT ALSO HOLDS. Repeated at the beginning of sections 28-33.
	BRADELEY. The only known place with this name in Pirehill Hundred.
11,32	WILGRIP. *Widegrip* is a misspelling of Wilegrip, 11,65, PNDB 407, cf. 405.
11,34	ROBERT HIMSELF HOLDS. Repeated at the beginning of 34-49, and 51-68. The change from *isdem* to *ipse* here coincides both with a change of Hundred and with the beginning of a new column.
	TOTMONSLOW. As in some other Staffordshire entries, the Hundred heading is placed after instead of before the first place named in the Hundred.
11,36	STOKE. The entry for Stoke-on-Trent, mentioned only here, is missing.
11,37	MADELEY HOLME. Also called Little Madeley.
	ENGLISHMEN HOLD. Room is left for one or two more strokes between *i* and *caruc.*
11,38	A. Marginal abbreviation placed against disputed tenure, standing for some verbal form of *adjudicatio, arbitratio* or other relevant word; see Hertfordshire 20,2 note.
11,48	...PLOUGHS. The *c* of *car* is written over a figure *i.* It may be that the regional return read *possunt esse i car* (1 plough are possible), and that the compiler noticed the error, but had no further information. 'It had' is a possible alternative to 'they had'.
11,51	ROBERT HIMSELF HOLDS. Repeated at the beginning of 51-68. The return to *ipse* coincides with the beginning of a different Hundred.
11,68	*MONETVILE.* Probably in Castle Church, near Stafford. The ending *vil(l)e* marks a recently established French place name; the prefix suggests that it may have been connected with Stafford mint.
12,2	WILLIAM ALSO HOLDS. Repeated at the beginning of 2-9, 11-12 and 18-21.
12,8	WOMBOURN. The writing avoids the reverse side of the repair in folio 249, see 11,27 note. The gap occurs at *Wambur/ne, saca/7 soca, servi/7 xiiii* and *ii/molini.*
12,11	WILLIAM ALSO HOLDS. See 12,2 note.
	CIPPEMORE. Probably between Enville and Kinver, VCH 54.
12,12	WOODLAND. *Silva,* not *silvae.* Dimensions not stated.
12,13	LOVETT. *Luuet* is the normal DB spelling of the French *Louvet* (wolf-cub), normally Lovett in later English (OEB 363), though often spelt Lovatt in Staffordshire. But since *Luuet* was an English free man before 1066, the spelling may represent a regional pronunciation of *Leuuiet* (Leofgeat), as with *Luuare* (12,27) for Leofwara. It is likely that two similar sounding names of different origins combined to give a common later form.
12,14	TWO...MEN. There is a gap equivalent to 3 or 4 letters between *duo* and *hoes* in the MS. WOODLAND. See 12,12 note.
12,16	'CROCKINGTON'. See 1,1 note.
12,17	SERVANTS. *Servientes regis,* the King's Servants (or 'Serjeants'), occur at the end of several counties, in a separate chapter, individually named, with or instead of the King's Thanes or Almsmen. Unnamed *Servientes* are also sometimes listed in villages, as, e.g. Leics. 13,63 (232d-233a) *Tra est vi car. In dnio sunt ii car cum i servo et xi villi et iiii sochi cum iiii bord et ix francig' servientibus habent x car int' omnes.* Though the Latin is ambiguous, the *Servientes* of Seisdon were probably, as in Leics., not in lordship. They may or may not be comparable with the west-country *radchenistre* or *radmans,* 'riding men', and may or may not have anything but the name in common with later 'serjeantries'.

12,18	WILLIAM ALSO HOLDS. See 12,2 note.

12,18   WILLIAM ALSO HOLDS. See 12,2 note.

12,22   THE ENTRY is duplicated in Warwicks. 27,6, where Godiva is omitted.

12,30   SIBFORD. In Oxfordshire.

12,31   DRAYTON. In Oxfordshire. The entry is a duplicate of chapter 57 of DB Oxon., except that the Oxon. entry begins *Turchil tenet de rege* (Thorkell holds from the King) and has its own listed heading 'Land of Thorkell'. NOW £8. The remaining three-quarters of col. 250 b is blank.

13,2   RICHARD ALSO HOLDS. Repeated at the beginning of sections 2-10.

13,8   VILLAGERS...HAVE. *Ibi sunt ... villani ... habent unam carucam; habent* perhaps for *habentes*.

16   NIGEL. Of Stafford, cf ED 5.

17,4   SHERIFF. Payment to the Sheriff here replaces the normal term *valet* (value). The amount, 12s on land for 6 ploughs, matches the later entries. Throughout the south-western counties, *valet* is replaced by *reddit*, pays, with the addition of *per annum* in the Exon DB. In Staffordshire, at Kingswinford (1,27 note), the Sheriff 'receives and pays the revenue of the manor' (*recipit et reddit firmam huius manerii*) (Worcestershire 1,5 .. col. 172 c). In 1136 Arnold, son of Vitalis of Hilderstone (11,27), granted part of his land, free of dues that concerned him *exceptis communibus geldis regis et communibus auxiliis vicecomitis et praepositorum hundredi et dominorum de quorum feudo ego teneo* (except for the King's common tax, and the common aids to the Sheriff and the Hundred-reeves and to the lords from whose Holdings I hold.) (Stone Cartulary, cited VCH 33).

17,6   PIREHILL. The heading is entered after instead of before the first place named in the Hundred.

17,19   VILLAGERS. There is room left for the insertion of *hnt .. car* at the end of the line. If such insertion were not intended, the meaning would be that the villagers were in lordship.

16   NIGEL. Chapter 16 is added at the foot of page 250 c, d, section 1 in 250 c, sections 2 and 3 in col 250d. In the MS, but not in Farley, the two portions begin exactly opposite each other. Chapters 14 and 15, in the bottom half of 250 c, above 16,1, are inserted in smaller cramped writing, with less space between words and between lines lines than on the rest of the page. Chapter 16 is entered with normal spacing.

16,1   CLIFTON. See also Derbyshire 1,25 (272 d) 'CHILCOTE...belongs to Clifton in Stafford'. Chilcote (SK 28 11, two miles east of Clifton) was transferred to Leicestershire in 1888, EPNS Derby 629.

16,3   MORETON. In Colwich, where Nigel also held from the Bishop of Chester, 2,18.

E   HOLDINGS ENTERED ELSEWHERE. The Latin text of these entries is given in the appropriate county volumes, from which the English translation is here excerpted.

EW 3   RUDGE and SHIPLEY are in the district that was in Staffordshire in 1086, but was transferred to Shropshire in the 12th century.

EW 4   SHIPLEY. See EW 3 note.

SYSTEMS OF REFERENCE TO DOMESDAY BOOK

The manuscript is divided into numbered chapters, and the chapters into sections, unsually marked by large initials and red ink. Farley however did not number the sections. References in the past have therefore been to the page or column. Several different ways of referring to the same column have been in use. The commonest are:

(i)	(ii)	(iii)	(iv)	(v)
152a	152	152a	152	152ai
152b	152	152a	152.2	152a2
152c	152b	152b	152b	152bi
152d	152b	152b	152b.2	152b2

In Staffordshire, the relation between the Vinogradoff column notation, here followed, and the chapters and sections is

246 a	B1 - Landholders	248 a	8,1 - 8,12	250 a	12,15 - 12,28
b	1,1 - 1,13	b	8,13 - 8,30	b	12,29 - 12,32
c	1,14 - 1,28	c	8,30 - 10,10	c	13,1 - 16,1
d	1,29 - 1,65	d	11,1 - 11,16	d	17,1 - 17,21
247 a	2,1 - 2,16	249 a	11,17 - 11,33		(16,2)
b	2,16 - 2,22	b	11,34 - 11,49		
c	3,1 - 5,2	c	11,50 - 11,65		
d	6,1 - 7,18	d	11,66 - 12,14		

INDEX OF PERSONS

Familiar modern spellings are given when they exist. Unfamiliar names are usually given in an approximate late 11th century form, avoiding variants that were already obsolescent or pedantic. Spellings that mislead the modern eye are avoided where possible. Two, however, cannot be avoided; they are combined in the name 'Leofgeat', pronounced 'Leffyet', or 'Levyet'. The definite article is omitted before bynames, except where there is reason to suppose that they described the individual. The chapter numbers of listed landholders are printed in italics.

Lovett	12,13	Swein	1,48;60. 8,8;20;24.
Earl Morcar	10,3		11,20;30
Nawen	4,9. 5,1	Tanio	11,28
Nicholas	16,1	Tholf	11,1. 13,4
Nigel of Stafford	16. 2,6-7;17-19;22.	Thorbern	1,46
	13,1-2;4;6. 15,2.	Thorgot	12,15
	ED 5	Thorkell	11,48. 12,26
Oda	1,47. 11,29	Thurstan	12,8;18;31
Ordmer	11,12;31;53;58	Toki	11,26
Osbern	11,30	Udi	17,2
Osbern son of Richard	7,2	Uhtred	1,50
Oswald	2,22	Ulfketel	2,22
Otto	17,19	Untan	12,23
Pandolf, see William		Urfer	11,14;51-52
Pata	13,5	Vitalis	11,27
Payne	12,14	Waga	12,25
Picot	2,6	Walbert	11,41. 12,7;17;23
Rafwin	1,41;45. 2,22. 11,30	Walter	8,9;26. 11,68. EW 2
Ralph son of Hubert	15	Warin	11,55-56
Ralph	10,10	Wihtric	11,10
Ralph	2,22. 12,8;30. EN 3.	Wilgrip	11,32;65
	EW 3-4	William son of Ansculf	12. B 8. EN 3
Ranulf	2,22	William son of	12,30. EW 5
Ravenkel	12,12	Corbucion	
Ravensward	ES 1	William Pandolf	8,19. ES 1
Reger (see Roger)	8,10	William	2,22. 8,20-22;28;30
Reginald Balliol	14. 8,4-6	Wivar	11,43. 12,26
Richard Forester	13	Wodi	1,52
Richard	17,16	Woodman	11,39
Richard, see Osbern		Wulfgar	8,9
Robert of Buck	15,1-2	Wulfgeat	1,58;59;64. 11,2 - 3;17;
Robert d'Oilly	8,32		19-22;28;33;36;38.
Robert of Stafford	11. B 6-7;12		17,10;19
Robert	2,3;22. 8,12. 11,42;	Wulfheah	1,43;56-57. 11,35;37.
	49-50;67. 12,6;9;		13,2
	18-19;24 - 25	Wulfhelm	17,15
Earl Roger (see Hugh)	8. B 4. ES 1. EW 1-4	Wulfhere	1,37
Roger	8,10-11;27. 10,7.	Wulfmer	1,62-63. 8,25. 11,2;5.
	12,11;21-22. ED 3		13,3
Saegrim	13,6	Wulfric	1,44. 8,13. 10,4. 11,14;
Samson	7. 7,1;13		27;29;34;51-52. 12,19.
Siward	11,15. ED 3		13,3. 16,3. 17,12-13
Sperri	17,15	Wulfstan	12,7;12;20
Stenulf	11,33	Wulfwin	11,47. 16,1. 17,10-11

Churches and Clergy

Abbeys			
Burton	4. B 3. ED 1-2	St. Mary's, Wolverhampton	7,14
Chester	10,7	St. Mary's, see Burton Abbey	
Westminster	3	St. Peter's, see Westminster Abbey	
Bishops		St. Remy's, Rheims	5. EN 1-2
of Chester	2. B 2. EW 5	St. Werburgh's, see Chester Abbey	
of Lichfield, see Leofwin		Stoke-on-Trent	11,36
Canons		Clerk	
of Stafford	6	Samson	7
of Wolverhampton	7	Priests	
Churches		see Alric, Edwin	
St. Chad's	2,5;10;15. 11,13	of Stafford	B 10
St. Evroul's	8,5;8-9	of Tettenhall	7,5
		of Wolverhampton	12,1

Secular Titles and Occupational Names

Countess (comitissa) ...Godiva. Earl (comes) ...Algar, Edwin, Harold, Leofric, Morcar, Roger.
Forester (forestarius) ...Richard. Sheriff (vicecomes) ...8,5. 17,4. 1,27 note.

INDEX OF PLACES

The name of each place is followed by (i) the initial of its Hundred and its location on the Map in this volume; (ii) its National Grid reference; (iii) chapter and section references in DB. Bracketed figures denote mention in sections dealing with a different place. Places marked with a (*) are in the 100 kilometre square lettered SK; those marked with a dagger (†) in square SO;with a cross (+) in square SP; other places are in square SJ. Since there is no Staffordshire EPNS volume, the documentary research that justifies the identification of places in most other counties is incomplete. Considerable research has been published by the Staffordshire Historical Collections, and is summarised and extended in VCH, volume 4 (1958). The editor is much indebted to Dr. J.P. Oakden for further advice. The Staffordshire Hundreds are Pirehill (P); Totmonslow (T); Cuttlestone (C); Offlow (O); and Seisdon (S). The National Grid reference system is explained on all Ordnance Survey maps, and in the Automobile Association Handbooks; the figures reading from left to right are given before those reading from bottom to top of the map. Places marked (S) are now in Shropshire.

Name	Code			Ref
Hill Chorlton	P 28	79	39	2,11
Cippemore	S 43	†82	85	12,11
Claverley (S)	S 19	†79	93	8,1
Clayton	P 21	85	43	13,6
CliftonCampville	O 31	*25	10	1,29. (16,1)
Codsall	S 1	86	03	17,1
Coldmeece	P 61	85	32	2,11
Coley	P 120	*01	22	2,17
Colt	P 122	*05	21	8,16
Colton	P 123	*05	20	8,15;(16).11,29
Compton	S 14	†88	98	1,2
Congreve	C 50	90	13	1,7
Consall	T 14	98	48	1,56
Cooksland	P 101	86	26	11,26
Coppenhall	C 24	90	19	11,63
Cotes	P 52	84	34	2,11
Coton (Stafford)	P 113	93	24	8,14
Coton Clanford	P 107	87	23	2,21
Coton (Milwich)	P 66	98	32	1,42
Cotwalton	P 54	92	34	1,45. 8,21
Coven	C 65	90	06	11,62
Cowley	C 17	82	19	1,7
Crakemarsh	T 41	*09	36	1,18
Creswell	P 103	89	25	8,19
'Crockington'	S 22	†84	94	(1,1). 12,16
Croxall	O 27	*19	13	ED 3
Croxden	T 34	*06	39	17,18
Croxton	P 70	78	31	2,14
'Cubbington'	–	–		8,4
Darlaston	P 53	88	34	4,6
Denstone	T 35	*10	40	1,55
Derrington	P 108	89	22	8,20
Dilhorne	T 21	97	43	11,41
Dimsdale	P 13	84	48	13,7
'Dorslow'	P 72	80	31	2,11
Doxey	P 110	90	23	2,21
Draycott	O 3	*15	28	10,5
Drayton (Penkridge)	C 36	92	16	1,7
Drayton Bassett	O 49	*19	00	1,30
Drointon	P 92	*02	26	2,19
Dunston	C 25	92	17	1,7
Church Eaton	C 18	84	17	11,65
Water Eaton	C 57	90	11	11,58
Eccleshall	P 76	83	29	2,10;(13;14;21)
Edingale	O 28	*21	12	ED 4;6
Elford	O 29	*18	10	1,26
Ellastone	T 28	*11	43	2,15. 11,39
Ellenhall	P 100	84	26	2,20
Endon	T 6	92	53	1,61
Enson	P 81	94	28	1,43
Enville	S 38	†82	86	12,10
Essington	C 71	96	03	12,22
Ettingshall	S 27	†93	96	12,18
Farley	T 24	*06	44	1,53
Fauld	O 5	*18	28	10,6-7
Featherstone	C 69	93	05	7,16
Fenton	P 20	89	44	17,21
Flashbrook	P 96	78	26	2,11
Forsbrook	T 22	96	41	1,60
Fradswell	P 67	99	31	2,8
Freeford	O 39	*13	07	2,22
Fulford	P 31	95	38	1,40
Gailey	C 58	91	10	11,59
Gayton	P 88	97	28	8,13
Gnosall	C 4	82	20	7,18
Gratwich	T 45	*02	31	11,35
Grindon	T 8	*08	54	11,3
Sheriff Hales (S)	C 37	75	12	B 4.-8,5
Hammerwich	O 36	*06	07	2,16
Hanchurch	P 24	84	41	13,5
Handsacre	O 18	*09	16	2,22
Handsworth	O 64	+05	90	12,29
Hanford	P 22	87	42	13,4
Harborne	O 66	+01	84	2,22
Harlaston	O 30	*21	10	1,32
Hatherton	C 61	95	10	7,13
Hatton	P 41	83	36	1,39
Haughton	C 5	86	20	11,52. (1
Great Haywood	P 116	99	22	2,5;(7-9
Heighley	P 10	77	46	1,36
Hilcote	P 77	84	29	1,46
Hilderstone	P 55	94	34	1,44. 11
Hilton (Wolverhampton)	C 70	95	05	7,15
Hilton (Shenstone)	O 37	*08	05	7,10
Himley	S 30	†88	91	12,12 -1
Hints	O 46	*15	02	2,22
Hixon	P 91	*00	25	2,6
Hopton	P 86	94	26	11,11
Hopwas	O 47	*17	04	1,31
'Horton'	–	–		2,22
Abbey Hulton	P 16	91	48	11,21
Huntington	C 54	97	13	13,10
Ingestre	P 114	97	24	11,32
Kingsley	T 18	*01	47	15,2. 16
Kingsnordley (S)	S 36	†77	87	8,2
Kingswinford	S 34	†88	88	1,1
Kinvaston	C 56	91	12	7,14
Kinver	S 44	†84	83	1,27
Knightley	C 3	81	25	8,6
Knighton (Mucklestone)	P 27	72	40	17,7
Knighton (Adbaston)	P 95	74	27	2,20
Knutton	P 12	83	46	13,8
Lapley	C 48	87	12	EN 1
Leek	T 5	98	56	1,21
Leigh	T 39	*02	35	4,7
Levedale	C 35	89	16	11,66
Lichfield	O 25	*12	09	2,16;22
'Littlebeech'	–	–		2,22
Littlehay, see *Colt*				
Littywood	C 23	89	18	11,6
Longnor	C 46	86	14	11,6
Loxley	T 44	*06	32	8,18
Loynton	C 1	77	24	11,53
(Great) Madeley	P 11	77	44	11,20
Madeley (Holme)	T 37	*06	38	11,37
Maer	P 36	79	38	11,17
Marchington	O 1	*13	30	10,4
Marston (by Stafford)	P 84	92	27	8,9
Marston (Church Eaton)	C 40	83	13	EN 2
Mayfield	T 27	*16	46	1,23
Meaford	P 43	88	35	5,1. 8,24

Place	Code			Ref
Meretown	C 14	75	20	1,24
Millmeece	P 59	83	33	1,37
Milwich	P 65	97	32	1,41. 11,30
Mitton	C 34	88	15	11,6
Moddershall	P 44	92	36	8,21
Monetvile	C 7	90	22	11,68
Moreton (Hanbury)	O 2	*14	29	10,8
Moreton (Colwich)	P 117	*02	22	2,18. 16,3
Moreton (Gnosall)	C 29	78	17	8,7
Morfe	S 37	†82	87	12,2
Moseley	S 4	93	03	12,21
Mucklestone	P 34	72	37	17,8
Musden	T 12	*12	50	1,50
Newton (in Blithfield)	P 93	*03	25	14,2
Newton (in Draycott)	T 31	98	39	1,58
Norbury	C 2	78	23	8,10
Normacot	P 26	92	42	13,3
Norton (Canes)	O 33	*01	07	2,16
Norton (-in-the-Moors)	P 9	89	51	11,19
Oaken	S 6	85	02	11,45
Oakley (Mucklestone)	P 33	70	36	1,35
Oakley (Croxall)	O 26	*19	13	11,47
Bishops Offley	P 75	77	29	2,11
High Offley	P 98	78	26	11,14
Ogley Hay	O 35	*05	06	7,11
Okeover	T 17	*15	48	4,8
High Onn	C 31	82	16	8,8
Little Onn	C 32	84	16	17,16
Orton	S 25	†86	95	12,7
Otherton	C 60	92	12	11,60
Oxley	S 7	90	02	12,9
Packington	O 41	*16	06	2,16;22
Patshull	S 9	80	00	11,44
Pattingham	S 11	†82	99	1,28
Paynsley	T 32	98	39	1,59
Pelsall	O 51	*02	03	7,9
Pendeford	S 3	89	03	12,20
Penkhull	P 18	85	45	1,16
Penkridge	C 51	92	14	1,7. 7,17
Lower Penn	S 24	†86	96	12,5
Upper Penn	S 26	†89	95	(B 8). 12,6
Perton	S 12	†85	98	3,1
Pillaton	C 53	94	13	4,10
Podmore	P 49	78	35	2,20
Quatt (S)	S 35	†75	88	EW 1
Ranton	P 104	85	24	11,25
Rickerscote	C 11	93	20	11,67
(Hamstall) Ridware	O 15	*10	19	5,2. 8,26. 11,50
(Mavesyn) Ridware	O 17	*08	16	8,17
(Pipe) Ridware	O 16	*09	17	2,22
Rocester	T 38	*11	39	1,17
Rodbaston	C 59	92	11	13,9
Rolleston	O 7	*23	27	10,3
Romsley (S)	S 42	†78	83	EW 2
Rowley	O 14	*12	21	2,16
Rownall	T 13	95	49	1,62
Rudge (S)	S 16	†81	97	EW 3
The Rudge	P 47	76	34	11,15
Rudyard	T 2	97	59	1,63
Rugeley	C 28	*04	17	1,22
Rushall	O 53	*02	01	12,26
Rushton	T 1	93	61	1,64
Rushton Grange	P 15	88	48	11,21
Salt	P 85	95	27	11,12
Sandon	P 83	95	24	1,13
'Little Sandon'	P 82	94	29	11,10
(Great) Saredon	C 66	95	08	11,61
(Little) Saredon	C 67	94	07	17,2
Sedgley	S 31	†91	93	12,1;4
Seighford	P 105	88	25	2,21
Seisdon	S 21	†83	94	12,17
Shareshill	C 68	94	06	11,64
Sheen	T 4	*11	61	1,51
Shelfield	O 52	*03	02	1,6
Shelton (-under-Harley)	P 29	81	39	1,38
Shenstone	O 38	*10	04	8,32
Shipley (S)	S 20	†80	95	EW 4
Shushions	C 41	84	14	17,20
Silkmore	C 10	93	21	11,6
Slindon	P 60	82	32	2,11
Smethwick	O 65	+02	88	2,22
Stafford (see Nigel, Robert)	P 112	93	23	B. 4,1. 6,1. 8,9;19. (10,9) 11,7
Standon	P 51	81	34	11,15
Stanshope	T 10	*12	54	1,52
Stanton	T 26	*12	46	1,49
Stapenhill	O 12	*25	22	ED 2;5
Stoke-by-Stone	P 63	91	33	11,9
Stoke-on-Trent	P 19	87	45	(11,36)
Stramshall	T 40	*08	35	17,17
Stretton (in Burton)	O 8	*25	26	4,4
Stretton (in Penkridge)	C 55	88	11	11,57
Stytchbrook	O 24	*11	11	2,16
Sugnall	P 71	79	30	2,20
Swynchurch	P 40	80	37	2,20
Swynnerton	P 42	85	35	11,18
Syerscote	O 44	*22	07	11,48
Talke	P 3	82	53	17,14
Tamhorn	O 42	*18	07	2,22
Tamworth	O 48	*20	04	(1,9;30)
Tean	T 33	*01	39	11,2
Tettenhall	S 10	88	00	1,2;(3). 7,5
Thorpe Constantine	O 32	*25	08	16,1
Thursfield	P 2	86	55	13,1
Tillington	P 111	91	25	11,1
Tipton	O 61	†94	92	2,22
Tittensor	P 38	87	38	11,33
Tixall	P 115	97	22	8,23. 11,31
Trentham	P 25	87	40	1,8
Trescott	S 17	†84	97	7,4
Trysull	S 23	†85	94	12,15
Tunstall	P 97	77	27	2,20

Tutbury	O 6	*21 29	10,1
'Tymmore'	O 40	*18 08	2,22
Tyrley	P 46	71 34	ES 1
Uttoxeter	T 42	*09 33	1,19
Walton (Grange)	C 30	80 17	8,11
Walton	P 78	86 27	2,20
(Eccleshall)			
Walton (Stone)	P 62	89 33	11,8
Walton	C 12	95 21	2,2
(-on-the-Hill)			
Warslow	T 3	*08 59	8,29
Wednesbury	O 60	†98 95	1,6
Wednesfield	O 55	94 00	7,7
Weeford	O 45	*14 03	2,22
Weston	P 87	97 27	17,15
(-upon-Trent)			
Weston	P 39	80 36	11,16
(Standon)			
Weston Coyney	T 19	93 43	11,34
Weston-under-	C 45	80 10	14,1
Lizard			
Wetmore	O 9	*25 24	4,3
Whiston	C 49	89 14	4,9

Whitmore	P 23	81 40	13,2
Wichnor	O 22	*17 16	11,49
Wigginton	O 43	*20 06	1,9
Wightwick	S 13	†87 98	1,3
Wilbrighton	C 15	79 18	11,54
Willenhall	O 56	†96 98	1,10. 7,8
Winnington	P 32	72 38	17,9
Winshill	O 11	*26 23	ED 1
Wolgarston	C 52	94 13	1,7
Wolseley	P 124	*02 20	2,7
Wolstanton	P 14	85 48	1,15
Wolverhampton	S 15	†91 98	7,1;(5)
Wombourn	S 29	†86 92	12,8
Woollaston	C 33	86 15	11,6
Wootton	P 99	83 27	2,20
(Eccleshall)			
Wootton-under-	T 25	*10 45	1,48
Weaver			
Worfield (S)	S 18	†75 95	B 5. 9,1
Wrottesley	S 5	84 01	11,46
Wyrley	O 34	*01 05	2,16
Yarlet	P 80	91 29	8,12
Yoxall	O 20	*14 19	2,22

Places not named

In CUTTLESTONE Hundred 11,51

Places not in Staffordshire

Indexed above, unless otherwise stated.

Elsewhere in Britain.
CHESHIRE Chester, see Index of Persons, Churches. MIDDLESEX Westminster, see Index of Persons, Churches. MONTGOMERY see Index of Persons, Hugh. OXFORDSHIRE Drayton 12,31. Sibford 12,30. SHROPSHIRE Alveley, Brockton Grange, Cheswardine, Chipnall, Claverley, Sheriff Hales, Kingsnordley, Romsley, Quatt, Rudge, Shipley, Worfield. WARWICKSHIRE Handsworth, Harborne and Perry Barr, now in Birmingham. WORCESTERSHIRE Arley.

Places outside Britain. (see Index of Persons)
Balliol (Bailleul)..Reginald. Bucy..Robert. Ferr(i)er(e)s..Henry. Hesdin..Arnulf. Oilly..Robert. Rheims..St. Remy' Church.

TECHNICAL TERMS

Many words meaning measurements have to be transliterated. But translation may not dodge other problems by the use of obsolete or made-up words which do not exist in modern English. The translations here used are given in italics. They cannot be exact; they aim at the nearest modern equivalent.

BEREWIC. An outlying place, attached to a manor. *o u t l i e r*

BORDARIUS. Cultivator of inferior status, usually with a little land. *s m a l l h o l d e r*

CARUCA. A plough, with the oxen who pulled it, usually reckoned as 8. *p l o u g h*

CARUCATA. Normally the equivalent of a *hide*, in former Danish areas. *c a r u c a t e*

COTARIUS. Inhabitant of a *cote*, cottage, often without land. *c o t t a g e r*

DOMINIUM. The mastery or dominion of a lord *(dominus)*; including ploughs, land men, villages, etc., reserved for the lord's use; often concentrated in a *home farm* or *demesne*, a 'Manor Farm' or 'Lordship Farm'. *l o r d s h i p*

FEUDUM. Continental variant of *feuum*, not used in England before 1066, either a landholder's total holding, or land held by special grant. *H o l d i n g*

FEUUM. Old English *feoh*, cattle, money, possessions in general, compare Latin *pecunia* and German *Vieh;* in later centuries, *feoff,* 'fief' or 'fee'. *h o l d i n g*

FIRMA. Old English *feorm*, provisions due to the King, fixed sum paid in place of these and of other miscellaneous dues. *r e v e n u e*

GELDUM. The principal Royal tax, originally levied during the Danish wars, normally at an equal number of pence on each *hide* of land. *t a x*

HIDE. A unit of land measurement, reckoned at 120 acres. *h i d e*

HUNDRED. A district within a shire, whose assembly of notables and village representatives usually met about once a month. *H u n d r e d*

LEUGA. A measure of length, usually a mile and a half. *l e a g u e*

M. Marginal abbreviation for manor.

PRAEPOSITUS, PRAEFECTUS. Old English *gerefa*, a royal officer. *r e e v e*

SACA. German *Sache,* English *sake,* Latin *causa,* affair, lawsuit; the fullest authority normally exercised by a lord. *f u l l j u r i s d i c t i o n*

SOCA. 'Soke', from *socn*, to seek, a comparable with Latin *quaestio*. Jurisdiction with the right to receive fines and a multiplicity of other dues. District in which such *soca* is exercised; a place in a *soca*. *j u r i s d i c t i o n*

SOCMANNUS. 'Soke man', liable to attend the court of a *soca* and serve its lord; free from many villager's burdens; before 1066 often with more land and higher status than villagers (see, e.g., Middlesex, Appendix 1); bracketed in the Commissioners' brief with the *liber homo* (free man). *F r e e m a n*

TAINUS, TEGNUS. Person holding land from the King by special grant; formerly used of the King's ministers and military companions. *t h a n e*

T.R.E. *tempore regis Edwardi,* in King Edward's time. *b e f o r e 1 0 6 6*

VILLA. Translating Old English *tun*, town. The later distinction between a small *village,* and a large *town* was not yet in use in 1086. *v i l l a g e*

VILLANUS. Member of a *villa*, usually with more land than a villager. *v i l l a g e r*

VIRGATA. A quarter of a *hide*, reckoned at 30 acres. *v i r g a t e*

NORTH STAFFORDSHIRE

PIREHILL Hundred
1 Biddulph
2 Thursfield
3 Talke
4 Balterley
5 Betley
6 Audley
7 Burslem
8 Bradeley
9 Norton
10 Heighley
11 Great Madeley
12 Knutton
13 Dimsdale
14 Wolstanton
15 Rushton Grange
16 Abbey Hulton
17 Bucknall
18 Penkhull
19 Stoke on Trent
20 Fenton
21 Clayton
22 Hanford
23 Whitmore
24 Hanchurch
25 Trentham
26 Normacot
27 Knighton
28 Hill Chorlton
29 Shelton
30 Barlaston
31 Fulford
32 Winnington
33 Oakley
34 Mucklestone
35 Ashley
36 Maer
37 Chapel Chorlton
38 Tittensor
39 Weston
40 Swynchurch
41 Hatton
42 Swynnerton
43 Meaford
44 Moddershall
45 Almington
46 Tyrley
47 The Rudge
48 Gerrard's Bromley
49 Podmore
50 Chatcull
51 Standon
52 Cotes
53 Darlaston
54 Cotwalton
55 Hilderstone
56 Broughton
57 Charnes

58 Aspley
59 Millmeece
60 Slindon
61 Coldmeece
62 Walton
63 Stoke by Stone
64 Aston
65 Milwich
66 Coton (Milwich)
67 Fradswell
68 Cheswardine
69 Chipnall
70 Croxton
71 Sugnall
72 'Dorslow'
73 Brockton
74 Baden Hall
75 Bishop's Offley
76 Eccleshall
77 Hilcote
78 Walton
79 Chebsey
80 Yarlet
81 Enson
82 Little Sandon
83 Sandon Hall
84 Marston
85 Salt
86 Hopton
87 Weston-upon-Trent
88 Gayton
89 Amerton
90 Chartley
91 Hixon
92 Drointon
93 Newton
94 Adbaston
95 Knighton
96 Flashbrook
97 Tunstall
98 High Offley
99 Wootton
100 Ellenhall
101 Cooksland
102 Bridgeford
103 Creswell
104 Ranton
105 Seighford
106 Brough Hall
107 Coton Clanford
108 Derrington
109 Aston
110 Doxey
111 Tillington
112 Stafford
113 Coton (Stafford)
114 Ingestre
115 Tixall

116 Great Haywood
117 Moreton
118 Blithfield
119 Abbot's Bromley
120 Coley
121 Bishton
122 *Colt*
123 Colton
124 Wolseley

TOTMONSLOW Hundred
1 Rushton
2 Rudyard
3 Warslow
4 Sheen
5 Leek
6 Endon
7 Cheddleton
8 Grindon
9 Alstonfield
10 Stanshope
11 Basford
12 Musden
13 Rownall
14 Consall
15 Cauldon
16 Blore
17 Okeover
18 Kingsley
19 Weston Coyney
20 Caverswall
21 Dilhorne
22 Forsbrook
23 Cheadle
24 Farley
25 Wootton-under-Weaver
26 Stanton
27 Mayfield
28 Ellastone
29 Bradley in the Moors
30 Alton
31 Newton
32 Paynsley
33 Tean
34 Croxden
35 Denstone
36 Checkley
37 Madeley Holme
38 Rocester
39 Leigh
40 Stramshall
41 Crakemarsh
42 Uttoxeter
43 Bramshall
44 Loxley
45 Gratwich

National Grid figures are shown on the map border.

NORTH STAFFORDSHIRE
Pirehill and Totmonslow Hundreds

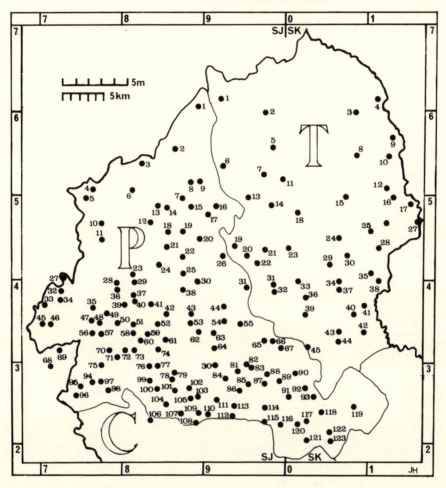

Each four-figure grid square represents one square kilometre,
or 247 acres, approximately 2 hides, at 120 acres to the hide.

SOUTH STAFFORDSHIRE

CUTTLESTONE Hundred
1 Loynton
2 Norbury
3 Knightley
4 Gnosall
5 Haughton
6 Billington
7 *Monetvile*
8 Burton
9 Baswich
10 Silkmore
11 Rickerscote
12 Walton-on-the-Hill
13 Brocton
14 Meretown
15 Wilbrighton
16 Beffcote
17 Cowley
18 Church Eaton
19 Apeton
20 Alstone
21 Barton-in-Bradley
22 Bradley
23 Littywood
24 Coppenhall
25 Dunston
26 Acton Trussell
27 Bednall
28 Rugeley
29 Moreton
30 Walton
31 High Onn
32 Little Onn
33 Woollaston
34 Mitton
35 Levedale
36 Drayton
37 Sheriff Hales
38 Brockton Grange
39 Brineton
40 Marston (Church Eaton)
41 Sushions
42 Blymhill
43 Beighterton
44 Brockhurst
45 Weston-under-Lizard
46 Longnor
47 Bickford
48 Lapley
49 Whiston
50 Congreve
51 Penkridge
52 Wolgarston
53 Pillaton
54 Huntington
55 Stretton
56 Kinvaston
57 Water Eaton
58 Gailey
59 Rodbaston
60 Otherton
61 Hatherton
62 Cannock
63 Brewood
64 Chillington
65 Coven
66 Great Saredon
67 Little Saredon
68 Shareshill
69 Featherstone
70 Hilton
71 Essington

OFFLOW Hundred
1 Marchington
2 Moreton
3 Draycott
4 Agardsley
5 Fauld
6 Tutbury
7 Rolleston
8 Stretton
9 Wetmore
10 Burton-upon-Trent
11 Winshill
12 Stapenhill
13 Branston
14 Rowley
15 Hamstall Ridware
16 Pipe Ridware
17 Mavesyn Ridware
18 Handsacre
19 King's Bromley
20 Yoxall
21 Barton-under-Needwood
22 Wichnor
23 Alrewas
24 Stytchbrook
25 Lichfield
26 Oakley
27 Croxall
28 Edingale
29 Elford
30 Harlaston
31 Clifton Campville
32 Thorpe Constantine
33 Norton Canes
34 Wyrley
35 Ogley Hay
36 Hammerwich
37 Hilton
38 Shenstone
39 Freeford
40 Tymmore
41 Packington
42 Tamhorn
43 Wigginton
44 Syerscote
45 Weeford
46 Hints
47 Hopwas
48 Tamworth
49 Drayton Bassett
50 Bloxwich
51 Pelshall

52 Shelfield
53 Rushall
54 Aldridge
55 Wednesfield
56 Willenhall
57 Bescot
58 Great Barr
59 Bradley
60 Wednesbury
61 Tipton
62 West Bromwich
63 Perry Barr
64 Handsworth
65 Smethwick
66 Harborne

SEISDON Hundred
1 Codsall
2 Bilbrook
3 Pendeford
4 Moseley
5 Wrottesley
6 Oaken
7 Oxley
8 Bushbury
9 Patshull
10 Tettenhall
11 Pattingham
12 Perton
13 Wightwick
14 Compton
15 Wolverhampton
16 Rudge
17 Trescott
18 Worfield
19 Claverley
20 Shipley
21 Seisdon
22 Crockington
23 Trysull
24 Lower Penn
25 Orton
26 Upper Penn
27 Ettingshall
28 Bilston
29 Wombourn
30 Himley
31 Sedgley
32 Bobbington
33 Chasepool
34 Kingswinford
35 Quatt
36 Kingsnordley
37 Morfe
38 Enville
39 Ashwood ?
40 Amblecote
41 Alveley
42 Romsley
43 *Cippemore*
44 Kinver
45 Arley

National Grid figures are shown on the map border.

SOUTH STAFFORDSHIRE
Cuttlestone, Offlow and Seisdon Hundreds

Each four-figure grid square represents one square kilometre,
or 247 acres, approximately 2 hides, at 120 acres to the hide.

ADDITIONS AND CORRECTIONS
HUNTINGDONSHIRE

Additions and corrections to earlier volumes will be printed as and when necessary. Middlesex and Surrey corrections appear in the Hertfordshire volume. The introduction warned that errors (chiefly of omission) were likely to be most frequent in the first three experimental volumes. The text is set under the supervision of the editor, not by the printer.

References are given to chapter, section and line. Words printed here in *italics* are to be *deleted*, those in roman type to be added or retained.

TEXT

B 12	See 19,9 note.		
1,9,5	*£40....face value.*	£5; now 10s less.	
2,1,6; 2,5,7;	Appendix; Index	*Thursten*	Thurstan
6,22,6	*their own*	this	
7,7 and 7,8 margin	*Delete M*		
8,2,5	*500 eels;*	500 eels; 5s;	
12,1,7	Add Hugh holds from Walter Giffard.		
13,1,2	*had*	has	
19,9	Add [HURSTINGSTONE Hundred]		
19,10	[HURSTINGSTONE Hundred]		
19,7,1	*2 3/4 hides*	2½ hides	
19,18,3	*16 villagers*	6 villagers	

19,23 margin   Lower 206 c by two lines, in the Latin and English.

20,6,7	*meadow, which*	meadow; which	

20,8   After line 3 Add

60 villagers and 8 smallholders who have 34 ploughs. A church and a priest;

25 Title   *Delete star (*)*

25,2 margin   Add M

NOTES

6,1   LAND. See 4,1 note.

6,13   ELTON. See also Northants. 6,9; 9,13 (221 b; 222 b).

13,1   KIMBOLTON. See Bedfordshire 17,2-3 (211 d). William of Warenne held TILBROOK, which adjoins Kimbolton, and was transferred to Huntingdonshire in recent times; and also *HANEFELDE*, which 'always lay in Kimbolton (lands), but rightly gave its defence obligations *(warra)* in Bedfordshire.'

19,9   BOTOLPH BRIDGE. The entry repeats B 12, with differing detail. Since the church was in the borough, the Ouse bridge linking Huntingdon and Godmanchester was evidently named from a chapel of St. Botolph.

19,12   CATWORTH. See also Northants. 6a, 24 (222 a), Peterborough Land. In CATWORTH Eustace holds 1½ hides. Land for 3 ploughs. 3 Freemen with 1 plough. The value was 10s; now 5s.

19,16   WINWICK. See also Northants 6a, 17 (221 d) Peterborough Land.
In WINWICK Eustace holds ½ hide from the Abbot. It is a
jurisdiction of Oundle.
  2 Freemen with 2 villagers have 2 ploughs.
The value was 5s; now 10s.
  Isambard and Rozelin hold 1½ hides from the Abbot; they belong
to Warmington. With 3 villagers they have 2 ploughs.
The value was 5s; now 40s.
  2 men-at-arms and 2 Servants with 1 Freeman hold 2 hides
and 3 virgates of land, which belong to Stoke (Doyle).
They have 2½ ploughs and
  8 villagers and 4 smallholders with 3 ploughs.
Meadow, 10 acres.
The value was 5s; now 50s.

    The three places to which Winwick land belonged lie close together,
between 5 and 7 miles north-west of Winwick in Huntingdonshire, but
remote from Winwick in Northants., 30 miles to the south-west.

    See also Northants. 55,4 (228 a), Land of Eustace.
Widelard holds ½ hide from Eustace in WINWICK. Land for 2 ploughs.
In lordship 1, with 1 slave;
  3 villagers with 2 ploughs.
Meadow, 3 acres.
The value was 10s; now 40s.
Aki held it.

20,6   EYNESBURY. See also Cambridgeshire 32 (30), 10 (200 c), Land of Picot.
In HATLEY Picot holds 2 hides...Picot states that he had 1 hide
of this land in exchange for Eynesbury.

D 19   *See note to chapter 4*   See Appendix

APPENDIX

Add   The Ely text is followed by a Summary. The figures agree with DB for three
of the Hunts. manors (Hamilton, p.169). But the Somersham figures are

	Ely Text	Ely Summary	DB		Ely Text	Ely Summary	DB
Lordship ploughs	2	3	2	Villagers	- -	28	32
Men's ploughs	20	10	9	Smallholders	13	13	9
(Totals)	(22)	(13)	(11)		- -	(41)	(41)

The three versions are of different dates. The Ely text reports what
Abbot Simon (or Simeon) 'found' (in 1082); the Summary was 'taken from the
King's records' *(secundum breves Regis)*; DB gives the 1086 Commissioners'
revision of earlier records. Unless there are figure mistakes, the number
of ploughs halved while the population remained steady.
The Summary also lists slaves (Somersham 4; Colne 3; Bluntisham 3;
Spaldwick 6), omitted in Hunts.DB. The figures suggest that slaves were
probably as numerous in Hunts. as in neighbouring counties, about 10%
of the village population.

INDEX OF PERSONS

Add   Brictmer Balehorn D 5; Abbot Simon, Abbot Thurstan, Appendix;
Isambard, Rozelin, Widelard, 19,16 note.

INDEX OF PLACES

Add   Barham, Easton, Long Stow, see Appendix; Tilbrook, 13,1 note
After   In Adjoining counties   Add   All these places, except Swineshead, are
also noticed in their own counties.

    Elsewhere in Britain. Add Boxted (Essex) D 7.